THE GAWLER
FOUNDATION COOKBOOK

A RECIPE FOR LIFE

DOROTHY EDGELOW

MICHELLE ANDERSON PUBLISHING
Melbourne

First published in Australia 2001
Michelle Anderson Publishing Pty Ltd
P.O. BOX 6032
Chapel Street North
South Yarra 3141
Australia
Tel: 03 9826 9028
Fax: 03 9826 8552
Email: mapubl@bigpond.net.au
© Copyright: Dorothy Edgelow 2001

Designed by: Helen Semmler
Photography by David Loram
Typeset by Midland Typesetters, Maryborough
Printed in Singapore by SNP SPrint Pte Ltd
Reprinted 2002

National Library of Australia
cataloguing-in-publication data:

Edgelow, Dorothy, 1930– .
The Gawler Foundation cookbook: a recipe for life.

Includes index.
ISBN 0 85572 304 1.

1. Cancer – Diet therapy. 2. Cookery (Natural foods).
I. Gawler Foundation. II. Title.

641.563

The author presents a three-day residential vegetarian cooking and healthy
lifestyle workshop based on the contents of this book. (For details contact the
Gawler Foundation on 03 5967 1730).

Acknowledgements

With deep gratitude and love I acknowledge the part played in my life by my immediate family who have paid me the honour of sharing their time here on earth with me.

To Lynette who had the courage to open the door and show us the path.

To Anne and Kerry who came too and supported us lovingly.

To Ken my husband who stood back but with open heart and chequebook helped us to travel.

To John, Philip and Chris, our sons in law, who joined us on our journey.

To our grandchildren Karen, Amanda, Glenn, Kathy, Shane, Erin, Kane, Kristy and Jodie for just being.

To my brothers and sisters who are always there if I need them.

To Grace Gawler for being an inspiration, for sharing her knowledge with me and helping to manifest this Centre of Light.

To Ian Gawler for his teachings and giving me the space and opportunity to learn and travel further down the path.

To Jo the chef who at a vital time in our life read somewhere and told us 'That food can help you get well'.

To Michael a great surgeon.

To Warren a doctor and naturopath.

To Gladys a lifelong friend for her friendship and dedication to feeding us during all our Apple A Day years.

To Peter who introduced us to another way of looking at life and to a meeting with Ian and Grace and their vision.

I would also like to acknowledge all the wonderful people who worked so hard in our Apple A Day Restaurants. Especially John, his wife Ingrid and mother in law Bep, and Margaret and her children.

From further along the path I would like to thank some very special people, not only for their help and friendship to me but also their dedication to the work they perform here at the Centre, giving so much of themselves, Glenda, Jennifer, Gail, Jill, Joy, Kerry, Maryannne, Amanda, Jodie, Ellen, Helma, Peter, John, Adrian and Tom.

We would not be able to provide the service we do here without the guidance of Bob, Nancy, Siegfried.

Not forgetting the very important people in the front line, Paul, Maureen, Carole, Aine, Vicki, Lisa, Rudi, Sheila, Jocelyn, Anne, Maureen and Robin.

A special thanks to Suzie and Jeff, Aine and Warwick for their love, support and guidance.

To my friend Christine for her generosity and for the lessons she provided.

To Vicki for her patience while typing this and to Michelle, our publisher, without her guidance you would not be reading this.

To all who played a part in my life, thus contributing to this book. Without them we would not have come this far.

Thank you.
God bless you all.

DEDICATION

To all our fellow travellers, who search for meaning,
for health, happiness and love.

Author's Note

The content of this book is based upon my own experience working with people and their diet over many years and presents my way of looking at eating habits and patterns in relation to health.

My early years of training were conventional and it wasn't until our daughter Lynette's illness that I looked seriously at food in regard to health.

In the last 22 years, 19 of them with The Gawler Foundation, I have seen the effect food can have on our bodies. The dietary principles recommended here are the result of years of personal observation of the many thousands of people who pass through our Centre.

We do not have a blanket or strict regime for all. People are encouraged to eat simple meals of organic and bio-dynamic foods, to take an interest in what they are eating and how they react to their choices using the guidelines offered. Our personal choices in food and lifestyle affect our health, we have free will, and these decisions shape our lives.

Miracles are always happening, every minute of every day only we don't generally recognise them as such. We take for granted all the wonders of this world and our body is one of those wonders. We think a great deal about what we put in our cars or our boats or any piece of machinery we own but do we care enough about the most wonderful complex piece of machinery that houses our soul, our body? This body that allows us to experience all that the blessed Creator, or whatever name you want to put on the energy that we are all small particles of, this body that we can learn so much from. This mind that can question and choose. We are given free will to shape our own lives but are we brave enough to accept that? We are all small particles of God, we are all one, we can all take responsibility for ourselves if we are brave enough, the only thing that can hold us back is our thoughts and we can control those. This planet and its blessings are ours to experience and enjoy, the miracle of ourselves is ours to unravel. We judge what is good or bad in our lives and react accordingly. God does not. Everything that happens to us is the right thing at the time, to lead us to the next step, to allow us to choose the path we are here to follow. Don't be afraid. We are all well loved and cared for, no harm will come to us. I would like to share with you some of the many miracles that although unperceived at the time, have given me the opportunity to be where I am now, in this exciting place where miracles happen all the time.

———————————

Dorothy Edgelow

Contents

Introduction

Why would you want to make changes to your style of eating and cooking? We need good reasons to make changes; they can be upsetting to our usual routine and to other family members. Changing this basic activity may be expensive and time consuming as well, but the benefits can be long lasting. Food is naturally associated with life and it is steadily being proven and accepted that it plays a part in how good that life is. So many shortcuts to having a meal are advertised now, that we might feel we are wasting effort by taking the time to prepare food. It appears that all the nutrients we need are added to almost all the food products we buy. But there is quite a difference between the way our bodies react to chemical additives in pre-prepared food, and the nutrients in fresh food.

There is also the most important fact that lovingly preparing a meal for ourselves or others does wonders for that food and its passage through the body. The vital elements of fresh food are enhanced or destroyed by our attitude to this activity. If you don't want to prepare a meal for yourself don't do it. Go without for the time being or let someone else do it. We gain nothing if we eat when we don't feel like it. Good food can turn to acid ash in our bodies if we are in a negative state of mind as we eat.

Our bodies are very like the soil and water; they respond in various ways to what is put into them. Our bodies can be too acid at one time, and too alkaline at another. Generally though if nature is left alone it will be in balance. As we control what goes on the earth we can certainly control what goes in our mouth.

Over the years, our food sources have been polluted with hundreds of chemicals making it even harder for us to be healthy. It takes a lot of thought and effort to combat the negative effect these chemicals have on our mental, emotional and physical bodies. The way we handle such problems shapes our lives.

Coming to these conclusions has for me been a wonderful, frightening, exasperating and blessed journey. I truly thank all of those who have taught me along the way, some with big direct input, others only in retrospect, but all bringing me to the point of putting experience down on paper—maybe opening a door a crack for someone else, or maybe just making the preparation of a meal a little easier.

Some people seem to have a big question around who they are and what they are doing here. To me it's very simple; try to look at each situation with an open mind. Whatever your choice it will be the right one for you, and will lead you to the next choice. Have faith and trust in a greater power guiding you, relax and count your blessings if you can.

Born in the early Depression years. I am the second of eight children, brought up on rice and rabbits in the Mallee. My mother told us often how hard it was to feed us. My father turned to building after being one of the Light Horsemen in the 1914–18 war. A good builder but not a good businesssman; we were always short of money and moved constantly all over Victoria and New South Wales, wherever there was work. A vegetable garden usually appeared when we were in a place long enough for something to grow. My childhood food seemed to consist of cabbage, tomatoes, onions, silverbeet and potatoes. Sometimes there was gravy beef or sausages. We had lots of dried legumes and I'm still fond of lima beans; there was always a filling steamed pudding or stewed fruit and custard. Plain simple food, which may account for all eight of us having nothing more serious in our lives up until now than varicose veins and associated circulatory problems.

By the age of ten I could cook a meal, by twelve I could make myself a dress. I loved to read and would sneak away to hide and read whenever I could. School was a blessing for me—a library to borrow books from and so much information to be had. I loved school and was awarded many books as prizes through the years. I was also awarded two scholarships to a city college, to learn to teach, but I refused to take them. The idea of standing in front of children and telling them what to do terrified me. Standing in front of adults doing that is even more frightening. The universe has a great sense of humour. If you dodge something long enough it goes full circle and catches you anyway.

I worked for a few years in a dressmaking business and married my boyfriend of two years. Ken was in the Navy, he was to be transferred to Darwin and I was to join him there when accommodation became available. In the meantime, I stayed in Melbourne and had a baby because my mother-in-law's advice on birth control did not work. She told me to put a band-aid over my navel; wrong place! In this instance ignorance was a blessing. I might not have had a wonderful daughter whom we called Lynette and who has taught me so much through her experience of cancer. I did not get to Darwin at that time of our lives. Instead I started my cooking career in earnest, first preparing food for my sister's wedding, and then doing that type of catering until starting my formal training.

We built a home and had two more lovely daughters, Anne and Kerry. Needing more money to finish the home, I began to work for a nearby pastrycook. As the only employee I was introduced to all aspects of cooking, and running a shop and business. I was there for nine and a half years. I left when my boss decided he wanted more than an employee. My husband Ken had progressed through the ranks at a large city hotel to become catering manager. At William Angliss school he learned to manage but not to cook. I worked in clubs, restaurants, hotels and catering establishments while our girls were growing up.

Life was pretty good and very interesting. I was working with a great Austrian chef, enjoying French à là Carte cooking and one morning, I started feeling very nauseated. Eventually I went to a doctor and was told I was pregnant. The doctor advised me to have an abortion as I had had quite a few blood clotting problems over the years. I was in my mid forties, our youngest child Kerry was seventeen years old, and the doctor considered pregnancy a bad risk at my age. It was a terrible decision to make. Abortion was something I was totally against. However, Ken was not enthused about another baby; we were

just getting to have a different life together with the girls on their own paths. So after advice from the doctor and a psychologist, I agreed to the termination.

I'm not sure of the sequence of events. In those days you weren't told much, apparently I bled very badly and received a blood transfusion and also injections to clot my blood. Ironic, when you think about the reasons given to me for not having the baby. The second day after the abortion I experienced very bad pain in my legs and was told my blood had clotted there and I had to have intravenous heparin and then warfarin for several more months. (Warfarin and heparin are anticoagulants.) I went back to work after a few weeks and more or less forgot about that experience.

One day while running along the path at a shopping centre, not looking where I was going, I ran into a street sign on a pole. I hit it so hard I knocked myself to the ground. I picked myself up, very embarrassed, rubbed my head and kept going. For two weeks after that my head ached slightly, and as I was not normally a headache person I went to the doctor again to be told I probably had a hairline fracture. Arrangements were made for me to have a scan at a local hospital. I was then told I needed to see a specialist as something strange showed up on the x-ray. The specialist did not do anymore scans. He just examined me and told me I needed brain surgery as I had a tumour in my head. He wanted me in hospital right away. I appeared disbelieving so he rang Ken at work and told him I had to do this or I would die. Arrangements were made for me to go into hospital in two weeks. Those two weeks were a nightmare. It was unbelievable that I was in this condition; only a slight headache. Wondering how I would be after, how things would change; would I be able to function as before. I could not come to terms with the situation at all.

The day before I was due at the hospital the doctor's receptionist rang to tell me he was going to America and they were referring me to another specialist whom I had to call to confirm an appointment. I think the powers that be were constantly looking after me.

The day came for the other appointment. I turned up at the hospital in a panic, and was given an injection of some dye by a man wearing a mask and leather vest. He had leather-like gloves on his hands and looked like something from another world. The injection made me feel ill. They put me on a bed, strapped down my body and arms and packed my head between sandbags. They took me into a blackened room. The bed was twisted and turned for what seemed a long time. Then came relief as I was unstrapped and taken off the bed. I rested for a while and went home. I was told to see the doctor again a week later.

The wait was awful. I think it was the only time in my life that I was bad tempered. Back at the hospital I was given the news that there was no tumour, only a funny shadow or hole. That was how the doctor described it; he did not know what to make of it but told me to go away and to come back only if I had bad headaches. I have not had a headache since. I am continually thankful that the first doctor flew off to America. It was quite a while too before my family, particularly Ken, stopped teasing me about having a "hole" in my head.

Several years passed; Lynette and Anne married and Kerry became engaged. Five months before her wedding I suddenly began to have difficulty walking. I had a lot of pain in my legs and also in my chest and back. A doctor said I had the flu and to take some aspirin. The next day I was in very bad pain and had difficulty breathing. Another doctor whom Ken had called announced I had an infection in my leg veins. Take this mixture and come and have your veins stripped when you feel better was his recommendation.

The next day I was wandering in and out of consciousness. Ken called a doctor again (three from the same surgery). This time I was put in an ambulance and sent to a city hospital for open-heart surgery. That is if I made it. Apparently my blood had clotted so much that the clot had passed into my lungs and was the cause of the pain in breathing. As well, there was a condition called thrombo phlebitis (inflammation of the veins).

It still amazes me that one can be so ill, so close to death and not realise it. This was brought home to me at the hospital. On arrival at the casualty ward there was a brief stop where two orderlies changed me from my home nightdress to a hospital gown. 'Be careful', one said as they undressed me. His mate replied 'Doesn't matter. This one's nearly gone'. I don't know why that came through so clearly to me. That they thought I was as good as dead really shocked me. Upstairs I went, to the intensive care unit to be attached to lots of machinery and monitors, with a heparin drip to stop the clotting.

At one stage I was up near the ceiling looking down on my body lying in the middle of the room on the bed. A couple of people were rushing about. I thought 'What am I doing up here, how come my body is still down there?' The panic, the feeling of having to get back into my body. I have to go home and finish making Kerry's wedding dress. There were two more bridesmaids' dresses to do and I had only half iced the cake. Somehow I arrived back in my body and asked the nurse to not let me go back to sleep please—thinking I had been dreaming.

Shortly after, I again found myself up above my body, this time moving off to a strange place full of Red Indians. They had long feather headdresses and seemed stiff and wooden. But they were very welcoming and wanted me to stay. Again I felt I had to get back into my body despite my interest in staying to find out what they were about.

Back into my body, and I was slowly improving when I was moved to a ward where a statue of Jesus on the cross hung right in front of me. Being there gave me lots of time to think about Jesus and God, what life was about, how much I enjoyed life and a determination to go home soon, although I was told that would take months.

There were several bad moments with clots breaking up and blocking things but I made it home in four weeks. I got on with the wedding preparations and went back to work, forgetting pretty much about those experiences in the hospital. I still had to go for weekly blood checks and take 15 mg of warfarin a day. The warfarin regimen went on for many years.

Life went on giving us great joy, through the four lovely grandchildren, Glenn to Lynette, Karen and Amanda to Anne and Kane to Kerry. When Kane was three months old he became ill. He had a high temperature and Kerry took him to a doctor who wasn't sure what the problem was and suggested she go home and wait. His condition became worse, so back to the doctor, this time to be told to take him as quickly as possible to a hospital. On the way, Kane turned blue and lost consciousness. Arriving at the hospital, emergency procedures to resuscitate him started and the staff on duty (it was Saturday night) had to guess what was wrong and how to try to bring this little body back to life. The only thing they could do was give him a huge dose of antibiotics while waiting for the arrival of a specialist who had been called away from a party.

After doing a spinal tap, pneumon-occal meningitis was diagnosed. Kane responded to the antibiotics, and drips were put into the side of his little head and into his arms and feet. This tiny body lay on a huge white bed for six weeks. Kerry expressed her milk and travelled each day on four buses to go to feed him. We had been told that if Kane lived there was a distinct possibility he would be mentally retarded or at the very least blind or deaf. As the boy grew we watched very carefully and were delighted to find that he was neither blind nor deaf and certainly not mentally retarded. He did have a very quick temper, but at the age of 22, and having experienced a few stormy years, has now grown to be a wonderful young man, developing emotionally and spiritually at a very fast pace.

A few months after this Lynette had another son, Shane. When he was six months old Lynette was diagnosed with cancer. Lynette had not been feeling well for quite a while, but the doctor put that down to the pregnancy, and then the birth and subsequent breast-feeding.

Lynette had continually asked for more tests but the doctor was not convinced she needed them. I found this amazing, as Lynette was very thin and very yellow. Finally she had a colonoscopy done and on ringing the doctor for a result was told to consult a specialist. She was not told by the original doctor what the problem was; I guess he must have felt guilty and was refusing to face her.

The specialist gave Lynette the diagnosis of probable bowel cancer and admitted her to hospital immediately for blood transfusions. She had to take her six-months-old son with her and to wean him as quickly as possible.

I can only imagine the thoughts that go through someone's head when given the news of cancer in their body. Lynette seemed more intent on weaning the baby and ensuring that he was OK. I guess it was a way of not having to face the cancer immediately. The pain of weaning the child so quickly would have distracted her attention from the oper-ation proposed.

The cancer had grown from the bowel, over the reproductive organs and to the liver and kidneys. Ken and I moved to Lynette and John's house to look after the children. I had given notice at work but as they needed me to stay till another chef was found. Shane spent quite a few days in his bassinette under the workbench in the kitchen of the club I worked for at the time; they were very considerate management there.

The operation to remove the cancer from Lynette's body was quite lengthy and she arrived back in the ward with a colostomy attached to her, and tubes running in and out of her body. The surgeon eventually spoke to us after he returned from a walk outside. He had gone out the SIC, told us because he was very upset at seeing such a mess in one so young. He had done his best but was not optimistic about her future. He said that as a rule the type of cancer that had struck Lynette usually allowed only about six more months of life.

During the four days of blood transfusions and weaning of the child, a book came to us. I can't remember where from. This little book gave me so much hope—in fact the only hope we came across for some while. It described many illnesses and their treatment, but underlying it all was the message that your attitude to yourself and your disease made a big difference to how well and how soon you recovered from your illness. I read this from front to back and raced to the hospital to show it to Lynette, saying, 'See you can get well, all you have to do is look at it the right way'. Thus faith is born. It all made so much sense. It was our first introduction to the power of the mind, although we didn't realise it at the time.

Another avenue of hope came a few weeks later, when the Austrian chef, Jo,

I had worked with, told me that he had read that food could make you well. This was a new thought. My training never mentioned food being used as a 'medicine'. Food was for tasting and looking good; no mention at all was made of nutrients.

Jo gave us a book written by Adele Davis, an American nutritionist, *Let's Get Well*. It gave details of treatment with food and supplements for many diseases. That book was all I had. The medical procedures in those days were surgery, radiotherapy, write your will, cross your fingers.

By the time Lynette came home from hospital I had managed to find a juicer and some of the recommended supplements. I made up a rough menu and regimen to follow.

Lynette remembers 'When I came home I had just settled into a chair when mum placed my baby in my arms. It was such a poignant moment. It still brings tears to my eyes 22 years later. In that moment I'm sure the determination to do whatever it took to get well again, to be there to watch my children grow up, was born.'

It was not easy to find information on how to heal cancer. I went into every health food shop and bookshop for miles around, buying anything that referred to cancer. I found a book on juices and their benefits, which was useful, and also one on fasting. Using these and Adele Davis's book, I started giving Lynette what was suggested to be a fairly alkaline diet. Green juice was a problem; it took so long to make one with a domestic juicer and then Lynette did not want to drink it. I had no clear idea of the combination of vegetable leaves and Lynette used to pull the sheets over her head when she saw a green juice coming. I used to wait till she was nearly suffocating, and she pulled the bedclothes down and then cajole her into drinking. Altogether she was fairly cooperative considering the change of foods.

I was experimenting all the time and some of the meals were not so pleasant. We were also using about 38 vitamins and other tablets three times a day. In retrospect it's a wonder I didn't kill her.

We had lots of green salads (chlorophyll for cleansing the blood and bowel), liver lightly cooked, and not much other meat. We used non-acid grains like millet and rice and I bought distilled water. Not a really great diet, but at the time it was a radical change from our usual way of eating. We certainly didn't get confirmation from others as to the benefit of what we were doing. One night, at about 3 am, when I was giving baby Shane his bottle, I began worrying about what we were doing. I wondered if I should stop and just let nature take its course, if I was interfering too much. But I couldn't just sit around and wait for Lynette to die. Suddenly, a very loud voice boomed from somewhere; 'Keep going, she will be all right'. My heart pounded. I put on the light but there was no one there. I eventually settled down and decided that whatever was the origin of that voice had to be good, so we kept on with our regimen.

Six or seven weeks after the operation, the radiotherapy sessions began. The doctors had wanted to hospitalise Lynette because they said the treatment would be so severe that she needed to stay there. Lynette didn't want to though, so we organised a roster of family and friends to take her back and forth for the treatment each day. At the end of the six weeks treatment, instead of being flat on her back, she was going on little Christmas shopping sprees. People used to ask Lynette how she was handling the treatment so well. We concluded it was all the vitamins and other things she was taking. We didn't know then of the effect that positive thinking and helping yourself can have on healing.

During these weeks too, we found a doctor who practised natural therapies. His name was Warren. This young man was a huge help to us. He sorted out all the tablets, those necessary and those not. He also arranged to give Lynette injections to boost her immune system. Lynette went back into hospital at her surgeon's request—he wanted to find out what was going on inside. He couldn't understand why she was so well and wanted to have a look. We had introduced Warren to him by then, and the surgeon allowed Warren to put vitamin C in the drip that was used during the operation. In retrospect it was similar in effect to the intravenous vitamin C now used so much.

The surgeon was very pleased and surprised that Lynette's insides were 'clean' as he called it. He removed the colostomy and rejoined her bowel. There was not a lot of conversation or explanation given in those days, so we just accepted his verdict, and rejoiced that the cancer was all gone in only four months. The hospital still insisted on Lynette having chemotherapy injections, which she did for several months; and which she handled very well—just a little nausea occasionally. No loss of hair, but she did put on some weight, which she was not so happy about.

Lynette's story

Given that my body was in such dire straits, the physical side of healing was the logical place to start, but I realised early on that it was only a part of the work I had to do. When asking the question, 'Why me?' the mental, emotional and spiritual aspects had to be addressed as well. So began a journey that continues today.

When I first met Ian Gawler, I found we had followed a similar dietary approach. But Ian had also looked at other areas, so a little while after he started his support groups I joined one. Meditation is important to him and the way he teaches helps relax the body, ease tension, and eventually brings peace to the mind. I recognised that I had put a lot of stress on myself by my attitudes and reactions to things going on in my life. I had difficulty in expressing my emotions and needs, always putting my own feelings second and doing what I thought was expected of me. I had a lot of negative thought and self-talk. I wanted to change people and situations around me, becoming frustrated when this didn't happen. By meditating and using visualisation and affirmations I was slowly able to make positive changes. I now realise I can only change myself and I try to accept others as they are, not how I want them to be.

I am much better at speaking out. I have learned to say no when that's appropriate and I have different priorities now. I have worked out what's important and what I can let go. I can now laugh at things I used to react negatively to. In hindsight, it seems incredible that I used to get so upset about things that really have so little importance. A lot is written about the mind/body connection, and looking back I can certainly see the connection in my own case. From what was going on in my head along with an inadequate diet, it was no wonder my body was struggling.

I became interested in learning how the body works, its mechanics, and to some extent the biochemistry of it. This led to a deep appreciation and a much greater respect for this wonderful vehicle we have been given. The more I looked into the workings of the body, its rhythms and cycles and its intelligence, the more I began to see the connnectedness of things, the things reflected in the world around me—nature.

I saw the simplicity and the complexity and these led me into the next and most important stage of my healing journey. While I was growing up, I attended Sunday school, church services and youth clubs and a Bible study group. But in my late teen years there always seemed to be more important or interesting things to do. The teachings stayed with me in the background, but I no longer took an active part in the church.

During my search for answers as to why I had developed cancer, my relationship with God, why I was here and what it was all about, were up for review. Several months after returning home from hospital, I went back to church, to try to make sense of it all. But I soon found that orthodox religion as it was being taught didn't have the answers I was after. Through my awakening appreciation of the human body and nature, I began to develop a sense of awe and wonder and a need to learn how it all fitted together. I seemed to be led from one group to another; from one book to the next—all adding to the overall picture I have today.

I am now much more at peace with who I am and why I am here. I appreciate and take delight in the simple things, particularly in nature, and I count my blessings daily. I now know that there is much more help available than I ever dreamed of. Through Spirit and by connecting to that Divine spark in me I

was able to heal myself in the truest sense of the word.

I still have my fair share of challenges, but I approach them from a different perspective and I handle them with much more grace. I have learned a lot over the last 22 years. I have had such help from my wonderful family and friends. I have done all I can to help myself as well as accepting help from those of the healing professions, both medical and complementary.

From talking with others who have been healed from cancer, I gather that my story is fairly typical. If you are on this journey I urge you to follow your instincts and more importantly, your heart. I am sure you will heal your life in many ways.

Lynette has enjoyed excellent health for many years now and has been an inspiration to family and friends alike. After doing voluntary work for The Foundation in the early years, Lynette went on to work in the office when it was established at Yarra Junction. Because of her own experience she was able to relate to those seeking help through The Foundation and was drawn to be more involved by working with the support groups. Later she became coordinator for those groups. It was not unusual for her to do home and hospital visits in her own time, offering encouragement and support to those who couldn't always get to the sessions at The Foundation.

In 1996 Lynette decided she needed to explore other avenues of service and left full-time work at The Foundation, occasionally going back to fill in for other staff members when needed. Her exploration over the years led her to run groups offering various healing techniques including meditation. Cutting the Ties That Bind, and Spiritual discussion groups as well as learning shiatsu massage, and reiki.

Lynette's search for the reasons she had been ill led her to look at fields like kinesiology, aromatherapy, reflexology, the biology and biochemistry of the body and many personal techniques aimed at clearing negative traits and strengthening the positive ones. Her work today, through the group she had founded 'The Heart of Light Healing Foundation', helps others heal their mental, emotional, physical or spiritual lives.

About ten months after Lynette's first operation she bounced into our home and told us she wanted to do something to help others with their eating habits. How did we feel about opening a small restaurant selling healthy food in a shopping mall being built near her home. We were excited about the possibility and looked into renting one of the spaces available. We spent frantic days looking for recipes and found none. We planned the layout and talked my brother David into fitting out the restaurant and takeaway food shop.

Fortunately, my husband, although he thought we were crazy, handed over his accumulated long service and superannuation money to get us started. With the additional help of Lynette's sister Anne and husband Philip (who had just sold a small business), and her other sister Kerry, we were ready for business when the shopping centre opened. It was exactly twelve months since Lynette was diagnosed with cancer.

We named the business Apple-A-Day, the notion being prevention of illness by eating better food. Apple-A-Day really struggled for some months. The new styles of food, juices, salads, yoghurt-icecream and wholemeal cakes were considered very strange and unpalatable by most. Our wonderful children worked without pay for some time and we all ate the leftovers. We experimented in the tiny space behind the shop but had many disasters, as this type of food on a big scale could not be prepared the same as at home. It was very different from my previous training and cooking experience.

During our early months at the shop we came into contact with people who were interested in looking at health in a different way. Lynette talked to many of them, to explain what we were doing. Many had cancer and had come to ask questions. We bought and gave away many of Adele Davis's books, as we still had not found any others with the same information.

Apple-A-Day struggled on for about six months, until suddenly we became very busy. In order to cope with the preparation and cooking, we decided to rent another shop space not far away and turn it into a kitchen. This meant more money, so we mortgaged our house. At the same time, the management of another new shopping centre asked if we would open a similar food outlet there. Our new kitchen was big enough to handle a large volume of produce and people, so we thought that would be a practical thing to do. The naturopath who had been helping Lynette and supplying tablets, also analysed our food. So now we knew how many nutrients there were in all our products which helped raise people's awareness of the value in the food they were eating.

Some people wanted to eat at our kitchen so we set up a part of that branch as a small cafe. We now had three outlets, as well as supplying twelve health food shops with take-away food. The staff increased to 27. We had to work two shifts in the kitchen, 4.00 am to 2.00 pm and 2.00 pm to 10.30 pm. There was very little time for sleep and Ken and I often went to a local motel instead of driving thirty minutes home. I sometimes wonder what the management of that motel must have thought of the middle-aged couple who arrived at midnight and left at 3.30 am.

We had a big struggle to get the last restaurant going as our naturopath friend who was going to supervise the proceedings and our merchandise was killed in a light plane crash just before we opened. We were devastated. He was such a brilliant young man with so much to offer. He left a wife and two small children and hundreds of mourning patients.

During all this time we and the kitchen staff were learning a great many interesting concepts from a young man, Peter, who came to work for us. He told us of Bach flowers, macrobiotics and of the Steiner teachings. This was all very new to us, and we listened with interest but still did not fully grasp the connections of all things.

We continued to work very hard. Kerry had joined us, bringing with her, her daughter Kristy who was three months old at the time. Kerry used to do the deliveries to our shops with little Kristy tucked in between the boxes of food. Anne had gone to manage one of the restaurants and Lynette was in another. Ken had left his job as catering manager at a city hotel and was our 'fix it man'. Kerry also kept our books and accounts and paid salaries. We had many wonderful staff who became firm friends, each contributing in a special way. Their support was truly appreciated.

One day a mass of large welts appeared on my left leg. They spread up to my knee and down to my toes. The skin rapidly broke down and in a few days my leg was a weeping red mass of flesh that was exceedingly painful and smelt atrocious. No doctor was able to help in any way. I even took time off to rest in a private hospital. The only possible cause suggested was an allergic reaction to the drugs I was taking to prevent my blood clotting. I had been told I would need to take them for the rest of my life. I now know 15 mg of warfarin per day plays havoc with your system. There was no option offered for this. I went along with it. I had been told changing the tablets would endanger my life. The thing in danger was my sanity. I tried everything to relieve the pain. I could not even count my toes, they were one jelled mess. I had to rebandage my leg at least twice a day and again on going to bed, sleeping on a hill of towels on top of the sheets.

For over a year I endured that dreadful leg, ruining many pairs of slacks and sandals, because of the constant weeping of the open welts. On going to bed one evening, I was determined to call a doctor the next day to arrange an amputation, I could stand the pain no longer. I was desperate. The pain never left, lying down, sitting up, walking or putting my leg up. I got out of bed as usual that morning at about 3.30 am to go to the shower. I unwrapped my leg and was astonished. It was almost normal, a little pinker than normal but all healed. Clear skin all over. I could not believe my eyes. I showered and rebandaged my leg, not trusting what I saw. I didn't say anything to anyone for several days. It was such a miracle I was afraid it would go away if I brought it into the light of day.

Several years passed and we had all become very tired. The long hours were catching up. So when we were asked if we would sell our Apple-A-Days, we agreed. The grandchildren all needed more time from their parents, and Ken was getting quite severe migraines. I knew it would be too big a business to try to run without their help.

During the takeover, Peter asked, 'What are we going to do now?' We had no idea. He suggested we go to see this man who was a customer of ours, who only had one leg and wore a kaftan, had recovered from terminal cancer and was running support groups to help others with cancer. Maybe we could help in some way. We went along to an afternoon session and were so excited to hear someone with so much information on healing, things we would like to have known when Lynette was so sick. We did the twelve-week course and decided to help Ian and Grace with their vision for a centre where they could help those affected by cancer. So began another learning phase in our lives.

In the early days before the committee of management was formed, we could only help Ian and Grace by supplying the cake and cookies for their groups and seminars. After we sold the restaurants, we made these in my kitchen at home. Making these cakes gave me an opportunity to get to know the type of food recommended; although it was similar to the diet Lynette had been using for many years.

In 1984 an opportunity came to

purchase forty acres of land next to where Grace and Ian lived. The need for a retreat centre to house the work was becoming more urgent.

The current committee was not comfortable with a purpose built centre so far away from Melbourne and there was no money to use for a deposit. The result was that the committee as a whole stood down and a new group was elected, myself included. It was agreed that the committee would raise the money to purchase the land at 55 Rayner Crt, Yarra Junction. Grace had told me that this was a special site. A place for healing. I went to have a look at the site and as I stepped out of the car at the top of the hill, a wave of feeling swept over me. It was hard to describe. Almost like an electric shock. I stood there for some minutes with a certainty growing in me that this was a very special place and I would do all I could for as long as I could to help this place to be used for healing, in whatever form that would take.

Fundraising for the deposit was very slow, so Ken and I put in $10,000 to make up the amount needed. David Bardas and Bill McHarg agreed to be guarantors. Finally the land was secured and a new era began.

We arranged car rallies, raffles, dinners, picnics, bush dances and anything that would bring in some dollars. Being the type of organisation we were, we had no Government funding. We did have a great group of supporters who were instrumental in eventually raising enough money to start the work up here to convert the old builder's shed to a useful space.

I was given the job of setting up the kitchen at the 'shed' and thoroughly enjoyed the activity. When we started serving meals I was very fortunate to have the help of some wonderful women. Gail, Glenda, Kerry, Jill, Joy and Mary-anne to name the core catering staff. Most of these ladies are still with us, providing wonderful food and assistance with the diet transition of our clients.

The Foundation's work continued to expand, now covering and offering programs for those affected by MS. We discovered that the principles used here are very beneficial in treating many other diseases.

Professor George Jelinek, who instigated our offering an MS program, and who has his own MS under control, has written a book on the subject titled 'Taking Control of Multiple Sclerosis'.

Grace Gawler, in 1984, also wrote an excellent book, 'Women of Silence. The Emotional Healing of breast Cancer'.

Ian Gawler's Medical and Work Related History—

including some of the philosophy at the heart of The Gawler Foundation's work with people affected by cancer

Ian Gawler is one of Australia's best known cancer survivors and advocates of a healthy lifestyle. His story offers hope and inspiration to people across the country. The self help techniques that he developed have helped many to convert hope into sustained health and peace of mind. A pioneer in Mind-Body Medicine, Dr Gawler is known for his clarity and good humour. With a gift for translating ancient wisdom into a modern context and having appeared widely in the media, Ian has played a major part in popularising meditation and other Mind-Body Medicine techniques in the western world.

Ian's own history, which is often misquoted, offers an example of the complex history of a long-term cancer survivor.

In 1975, as a young veterinarian and decathlon athlete, aged 24, Ian had his right leg amputated because of osteogenic sarcoma (bone cancer). Later that year inoperable secondaries were confirmed in the right inguinal and mediastinal lymph nodes. In those days, he was told available chemotherapies were of no value and radiotherapy would be palliative at best. The prognosis of 3-6 months was considered reasonable. Ian, therefore, turned to diet, meditation and other self-help techniques.

Ian had the belief that cancer involved a failure of the body's natural defenses including the immune system. He felt that if it was possible to find a way to reactivate the body's inner capacity for healing, then perhaps he could recover.

Initially Ian followed the Gerson

Diet.[1] This was exceedingly rigorous and despite full support from his first wife Grace, it created many problems. These days, Ian does not advise using the Gerson Diet as for most people it is extremely demanding in a home setting. However, he does believe it has enough merit to warrant serious study.

Ian feels sure that nutritional factors helped him a great deal. Many patients report the positive benefits associated with changing their diets. There is a good body of evidence to indicate that nutrition can alter the outcome of cancer. Numerous animal studies confirm the proposition, and while studies in humans have been more limited, in breast and prostate cancer specifically there is strong evidence that diet indeed can be curative.

In response to his cancer, Ian also began meditation with the Melbourne based, and now deceased psychiatrist, Dr Ainslie Meares. Dr Meares believed that prolonged meditation could reduce cortisol levels, improve immune function and so lead to recovery.[2]

For the first three months after the diagnosis of secondaries, Ian's tumours remained static. Then severe sciatic pain forced him to try acupuncture (two treatments only) then palliative radiotherapy (three treatments to his lower lumbar region only). The pain continued to be severe but was then relieved by injections of a mistletoe extract (Plenisol) administered by a GP interested in natural therapies.

By March 1976, Ian was suffering severe weight loss (though 1.8m he weighed 40kg), jaundice, night sweats and hydronephrosis (obstruction) of the right kidney. The pain was again severe.

At this point Ian's surgeon considered his prognosis to be a couple of weeks.

Ian then left for four weeks with faith healers in the Philippines. This was a truly extraordinary experience which challenged all Ian's preconceptions and experience of surgery. Importantly he came home 6kg heavier, with no pain and feeling he had turned the corner.

In the next six months, while Ian's general health improved, the cancer itself continued to spread and grow. He maintained the modified diet and meditation while Grace did many hours of massage for him. They also investigated and experimented with many natural therapies.

By late 1976 Ian had massive secondaries on his sternum (photographs of these are in the back of Ian's book 'You Can Conquer Cancer'), left lung, lumbar spine, mediastinal and inguinal lymph nodes. Remarkably, he was free of pain and otherwise unaffected by this

---

1 Gerson, M.A. *Cancer Therapy—Results of 50 Cases*, The Gerson Institute, Bonita, 1958.
2 Meares, A. *The Medical Journal of Australia*, 1983, June, 583-84.

widespread cancer. However, Ian reconsidered the medical options.

He was offered experimental chemotherapy based on adriamycin, vincristine and methotrexate. Ian completed the first round of this protocol in two and a half months but there was little change in his tumour sizes. He then elected to cease treatment despite warnings of a rapid rebound in the tumour's growth.

Ian returned to the Philippines for three months, travelling then to India. In May 1977, the holy man Sai Baba told Ian: 'You are already cured, don't worry.'

This was another major turning point, as it helped him to dispel doubts and be fully confident of recovery.

Ian had no more medical treatment but continued, fully committed, to the self-help regimen as described.

By June 1978 all visible lesions had subsided. Medical tests in Adelaide confirmed that there was no evidence of active cancer, but that he did have TB! He responded rapidly to standard TB treatment, and his case was reported by Meares.[3]

Ian and Grace moved to Yarra Junction, Victoria in 1980. They had four children after Ian's chemotherapy. Grace ceased working at The Foundation at the end of 1996 and she and Ian separated at the end of 1997.

In 2000 Ian married Ruth, now Dr Ruth Gawler, a General Practitioner who had been living and working in Alice Springs. Ruth has a special interest in Mind/Body Medicine, counselling and holistic techniques. She has a Masters in General Practice Psychiatry and has been working with Ian since 2001 leading programs and providing counselling at The Foundation.

Obviously Ian's is a complex history. Ian is often asked what cured him, and replies that it was a combined result. Ian has no doubt that the medical treatment on its own would have been unsuccessful. His recovery demanded a great deal of effort from both himself and from Grace. Rather than just one thing in particular, it seemed that many useful things had combined to produce such a spectacular result.

In 1981, Ian and Grace began an innovative cancer support group based upon his experiences. At that time little was being offered to people affected by cancer who wanted to help themselves. Patients were being left to fend for themselves. Hope was often denied and the myth of cancer as a death sentence prevailed.

Ian was keen to redress these painful problems and felt that he had something important to offer. The main ingredients of his approach were (and still are) good nutrition, developing a positive state of mind, meditation and mutual support.

These patient-based cancer self-help programs gained wide interest.

---

3 Meares, A. *The Medical Journal of Australia*, 1978, 2-433.

In 1983 a non-profit, non-denominational charitable organisation was founded to extend this work and Ian left his veterinary practice.

In 1984 Ian detailed his approach in *You Can Conquer Cancer*.[4] The book was launched by Sir Edward 'Weary' Dunlop who remained a strong supporter of this work. The book has sold over 100,000 copies in Australia and a new, completely revised edition was released in 2001.

Also, in 1984, being keen on scientific evaluation, Ian unsuccessfully approached the Peter MacCallum Cancer Institute in Melbourne and the Victorian Anti-Cancer Council for help with research. Like many self-help groups, The Foundation's resources were limited and could get no outside assistance for research at that time.

In 1987, The Foundation began developing its own extensive in-house database with a view to follow-up research. In the same year Ian was awarded the Order of Australia medal for services to the community and published a detailed account of his meditation and positive thinking methods in the book *Peace of Mind*.[5]

In 1988 on the ABC's *Couchman Across Australia*, Professor Ray Lowenthal challenged Ian to present his 50 best cases for assessment. Ian readily agreed, but the proposal lapsed when Professor Lowenthal was unable to secure funding for the research from the Australian Cancer Foundation.

The Foundation is now co-operating on a major research project with Swinburne University, has helped fund a major study with the Royal Melbourne Institute of Technology and continues with its own in-house research projects.

The Foundation welcomes both prospective participants and medical visitors to our programs and many doctors have attended as patients, partners or observers. These people see what can be accomplished.

Remarkable transformations occur when people attend an active cancer self-help group. The hope, energy and vitality in these groups is truly amazing and quite inspiring.

People learn to communicate, to balance their lives, to clarify their goals and to work effectively towards them.

The Foundation uses strategies in its programs to help people avoid guilt and to find the peace of mind that is a major focus of Ian's work.

At The Foundation, we never say we can cure cancer. We believe that it is possible for people to learn how to cure themselves. Our self-help programs' stated intention is to help cancer-affected people improve their quality of life and

4 Gawler, I.J. *You Can Conquer Cancer*, Michelle Anderson Publishing Pty Ltd 2001.
5 Gawler, I.J. *Peace of Mind*, Michelle Anderson Publishing Pty Ltd 2002.

contribute wherever possible to their own survival. People learn to live well and to die well—when their time does come. There have been many cases of remarkable recovery where people have survived against the odds.

The self-help approach augments conventional therapies and, at the very least, plays a vital role in meeting the human needs of everyone affected by cancer.

There is a widespread feeling that doctors need to attend better to the psychological and spiritual needs of their patients. We have a system that has been doing this effectively for more than 21 years and happily share it.

When Ian began this work in 1981, the whole area was unexplored. Now support groups are coming into most cancer hospitals and patients are seeking the self-help options.

The Foundation's approach has always been to encourage cooperation and communication between patients and doctors. Best results are obtained when doctors work with patients and their families in partnership.

Many doctors do refer their patients to The Foundation and many more encourage their patients to include self-help techniques as part of their healing equation. We believe good doctors always have done so, and hope more doctors will have the confidence to support patients and families effectively in these self-help efforts.

The Foundation's aim is to provide information that is available in a balanced way, encouraging individuals to take responsibility for their own decisions. We then support people actively as they work towards healing, good health and wellbeing.

The Foundation's 12 week cancer self-help program has been running continuously since 1981. The ten-day residential program, 'Life & Living', for people affected by cancer was commenced in 1985. These programs have evolved constantly in response to feedback from those attending, new research and the ongoing experience of our group leaders. The groups, the teachings and the support The Foundation provides, are all based upon the expressed needs of people affected by cancer—the patients, the partners, the friends and carers. We aim to help people to feel better and to live longer!

The crucial question is: why do some patients recover when others with the same illness do not? At The Gawler Foundation, we are confident that there is more to this than just good luck. Finding out what makes the difference, what people can do to make a difference, is what we are most interested in studying and what new patients are interested to learn about.

We suggest that it is possible to learn from successful patients, just as we could learn from successful sporting or business people.

After 21 years, and having helped well over 12,000 people through the groups we have run, all of us at The Foundation know we have the experience and the expertise to help and are committed to doing so. If you feel that we can be of help to you or someone you love, please do contact The Foundation. (See the contact details at the back of the book.)

THE GAWLER FOUNDATION PROGRAMS

The Foundation conducts programs in Melbourne and at its Headquarters and residential centre in the beautiful Upper Yarra Valley. The Centre—called the Yarra Valley Living Centre—is spacious modern and comfortable. Set amidst 40 glorious acres of rolling woodland and forest, it backs onto the tranquil little Yarra River. The Centre is a haven for native animals and birds and provides a wonderful environment for peace and healing.

Accommodation includes twins with and without ensuites and more basic shared rooms. The healthy, delicious meals are a renowned feature of the programs and are a direct translation of the principles in Ian's 'You Can Conquer Cancer' and the recipes in this book. The food is organic or biodynamically produced wherever possible and much comes from The Foundation's own delightful garden. The diet is vegetarian, dairy free, fresh, abundant and vital. A great range of herbal teas and coffees compliment what is truely gourmet healthy food. It looks and tastes wonderful! Fresh juices are another feature of the healing programs.

A summary of the care programs at The Foundation follows. For more information you can call The Foundation Staff directly on (03) 5967 1730 or visit the website: www.gawler.org.

TEN DAY RESIDENTIAL

Our bodies have a natural, inherent capacity to heal themselves. The principles that are explored in this program will enable you to activate and develop that healing power, maximising your body's potential to restore its natural state of balance and vitality. These principles include relaxation and meditation, a positive state of mind, good diet and nutrition, overcoming obstacles to peace of mind, finding meaning and purpose in life and drawing upon effective support.

This self-help approach is intended to work with and reinforce effective medical treatments as well as relevant complementary therapies.

The residential programs began in 1985. Over 6,000 people have attended. This provides an amazing pool of shared knowledge, experience and diversity—from teenagers to eighty-year-olds, from all walks of life, united by a common challenge. You can learn what has worked for many others and will be helped to apply it in your own life.

The program requires a good deal of energy to benefit fully from attending, you need to be able to join in. It is also important to read Ian's books before attending this program (You Can Conquer Cancer, Peace of Mind, Meditation Pure and Simple, The Creative Power of Imagery). The Gawler Foundation staff all draw on a rich background of personal experience and training to facilitate these programs.

Most sessions involve learning through direct participation and experience. Discussion is encouraged and there is plenty of time for questions and answers. You can meet and share with a group of wonderful, exceptional people.

HEALTH, HEALING & BEYOND

The Five Day Follow Up Program, Health, Healing & Beyond is suggested as a refresher course for those who have done the Ten Day Program or the 12 week cancer self-help program. Health, Healing and Beyond has an informal and flexible format. A questionnaire is used to help identify the needs of each participant. Then each program is tailored to meet those specific needs.

The program offers the opportunity for participants to refocus and go deeper into their healing process, to address any issues and obstacles they may have come up against, and to learn some new techniques. A major feature is the guided imagery work that introduces participants to techniques that draw upon their inner wisdom and help them to develop insight and clarity.

THE 12 WEEK CANCER SELF HELP PROGRAM

This unique Cancer Self-Help Group offers a twelve week program based on the material in Ian's book, 'You Can Conquer Cancer'. It provides an opportunity to learn and discuss self help techniques in a mutually supportive, positive and caring environment.

At The Foundation, we recognise that support people, the relatives and friends of cancer patients, are often faced with major challenges of their own. What will happen? what can I do? am I doing enough and doing it right?—all these are very urgent questions for support people.

The Foundation's programs are tailored to assist support people as well as patients, as they recognise the key role of both. Hence it is recommended that support people attend the groups and utilise the counsellors when needed. There is a specific Carer's Group during the last week of each month.

INWARD BOUND

This is a Five Day Live In Program for people with a variety of needs. Developed by Ian Gawler and Paul Bedson, 'Inward Bound' is a gently introspective, meditation-based stress management, regeneration and personal development program.

Amidst a busy modern lifestyle, many people recognise the need for some time out. Time for yourself and time to reconnect with the essence of life—your own inner wisdom and strength.

MEDITATION RETREATS

These retreats are designed to create harmony of the body, mind and spirit. They provide a time to journey inward, to help you learn and practise techniques that will deepen your experience of meditation and to get to know your true self more closely. The focus is mainly experiential, with some discussion, and the telling of stories.

During the program you can journey inward and explore meditation and creative imagery. These remarkable techniques can provide direct access to your inner wisdom and help you to manage stress, to relax, to let go a little and to find balance, meaning and peace of mind. Many of the techniques in Ianís books will be practised and experienced directly.

INDIVIDUAL MEDITATION INSTRUCTION

Some people find it challenging to get started with meditation just from reading a book or listening to a tape.

Personal contact with an experienced meditation instructor can help you to commence or to clarify obstacles that have been hindering your meditation practice. Direct tuition and feedback from a teacher can prevent confusion and frustration about meditation techniques.

These individual sessions can make meditation clear and simple and achievable for everyone.

COUNSELLING SERVICES

The counsellors available at The Gawler Foundation are highly qualified in all aspects of general counselling.

As well, they are trained and experienced in working with people (patients and family members) who are living with the challenges associated with a life-threatening illness, especially cancer.

HOME AND HOSPITAL-BASED COUNSELLING

A counselling service for cancer patients and their families is available for people who are not well enough to travel to our venues at Yarra Junction or Melbourne. Arrangements can be made with one of our counsellors, to visit clients at their home or in hospital.

Gawler Foundation Dietary Principles and Practice

The principle behind The Foundation's choice of diet is to take into our bodies food that is good for us. We do not eat dead or useless filling foods or foods that are grown and covered with chemicals. Our bodies have to cope with many external pollutants, but we can control what goes in our mouths. We give our bodies a very definite message when we eat what we know is good for us. We can all be responsible for our own health and we should take an active part in deciding what to eat.

Organically grown fruit, vegetables and grains are readily available. Bio-dynamically produced foods are too, and the effort should be made to obtain them. We thereby make a definite effort to regain our health, from the mind through to the body.

When vegetables are grown well, they contain special enzymes that help to cleanse and build up the body. Serve grains with vegetables for complete nourishment, eating those that grow locally and in season if you can. Eating vegetables raw or juiced gives us certain nutrients, and cooking them allows us to access other properties not released when they are raw. A combination of two-thirds raw and one-third cooked is generally good. If you are not comfortable eating so much raw food, increase your cooked food and drink raw juices.

Keeping your meals fairly simple, with not too many different ingredients in each meal helps. Better absorption and nutrition come with simple meals. If you cannot tolerate a lot of raw food, fresh juices can supply the enzymes and vital forces usually gained through eating raw food. A few changes we can make quite easily in our kitchens help to eliminate unhealthy products and procedures.

I have some knowledge of the chemical and nutritional content of food, but having no medical degree I will not discuss here food to be used as medicine. I will confine myself to the reasons for the dietary practices recommended by The Foundation.

Our bodies need to be in a state of acid

and alkaline balance (yin and yang in Chinese medicine), in order to be healthy. Animal foods, sugars and fats are generally acid forming. Vegetables, grains and fruits are usually alkaline forming. All natural foods contain both acid and alkaline-forming elements. If possible eat food close to its natural form. It is not the organic matter but the inorganic matter of foods that leaves acid residue in the body. High protein foods are usually processed, and animal foods are generally acid forming. Most grains can be acid forming unless they are chewed very well. Chewing, by adding ptyalin from the saliva to the grain, in turn changes the acid elements to alkaline.

Apart from food, our bodies are affected by our thoughts. There is a great deal of information about mind and body interaction, but in this book I will just say this; negativity, anger, resentment and unhappiness all affect how our bodies cope with food. Even the right type of food can be turned into acid ash by these emotions. Try to relax and think calm happy thoughts when preparing and eating your meals.

If obtaining good organic food is worrying and taxing, buy the best fruit and vegetables you can and wash them in a solution of vinegar and water 1:100. Tell your body you are doing the best you can.

Here at the Centre we sit for a few moments of silence before each meal. We do not say a formal grace as it is not appropriate for everyone. Just take a moment or two to bless your food, be thankful for what you have and be positive that what you are eating and doing will help you to health.

Many patterns of using food derive the maximum benefit for each individual need. Sometimes cooked food is most needed for a particular state you are in. At other times raw food seems better. Everyone is unique and it can be a fascinating experience learning about your body's needs and being comfortable choosing what suits you best. Only you know how you feel. Along the way you realise the part your food plays in your overall well-being. Delve a little into all the different aspects of yourself and food and how you feel after eating certain foods. It gives you an insight into what approach to diet is best for you.

Take a look at Chinese principles and how the organs relate to one another. Taking a look at the chemistry of food, at the nutritional aspect and getting to know and trust your own instincts is a marvellously liberating act. Buying, preparing and eating your good food should be a pleasure, not a chore. Find a way to enjoy it and you are well on the way to health.

Remember that what you put in your mouth is only part of the way to a healthy life. You must match it up with the other parts of your life. Sort out past and present relationships with yourself and others. Sort out your emotional state and your spiritual beliefs and what has put you where you are. Accept that you are not expected to know everything, and that your experiences are happening at the right time. There is no wrong time. We judge things to be right or wrong, good or bad. God does not. We feel guilt and judge others and ourselves. God does not.

Certified Organic Foods—Why and what are they?

Organic food means food that has been produced using organic farming methods, and foods that have received minimal processing. Organic foods are grown without the use of pesticides, antibiotics, hormones, artificial fertiliser, genetic manipulation, nor any unnecessary exposure to environmental pollution. Even after the correct farming or growing procedures are practised, it takes a few years to be able to label produce certified organic.

Although washing produce in a vinegar solution does remove the outside sprays, a lot of damage is done to the actual seed before it gets in the ground. For example, a non-organic apple may have been dosed with up to 100 additives before you get to eat it. Broccoli generally has been sprayed with 32 chemicals. More than 50 per cent of all pesticides sprayed on fruit and vegetables are there merely to improve its appearance. Organically grown food is sometimes smaller and less attractive, with a few blemishes, but the flavour and nutrient content are far superior.

Some of the chemicals used to spray crops have been linked to allergies and cancer. Some are associated with Irritable Bowel Syndrome, Candida and Inflammatory Bowel Disease and lowered fertility problems. Apart from being better for our health, organic farming is better for our planet too.

What is biodynamics?

Biodynamics is an advanced form of organic agriculture, which was introduced by Dr Rudolf Steiner in 1924. Dr Steiner was an Austrian scientist/ philosopher who had deep insight into nature and into many areas of human endeavour. He gave detailed suggestions for a renewal of agriculture in a series of lectures given to farmers in 1924. He insisted that all his suggestions had been fully tested and scientifically validated. This sound scientific basis continues to be an important feature of biodynamics today.

The method spread rather slowly worldwide. In the 1950s Alex Podolinsky made it applicable to large acreage and small workforce farms in Australia, thus appealing to the many professional farmers who felt morally ill at ease with the use of artificial fertilisers and poisonous sprays. Podolinsky's group, the Bio-dynamic Agricultural Association of Australia, is now the largest natural farming body anywhere. Members produce every type of farm product grown in Australia on farms totalling over a million hectares.

Biodynamic methods and equipment created in Australia are now used in many countries and Alex advises farmers in Europe, Scandinavia, the Ukraine, America and South Africa.

Biodynamic features
500 is a substance made from specially treated cow manure. It is liquified and sprayed on the soil twice a year. It creates a powerful soil structure, promoting humus formation and root growth.

Companion planting—different plant species interact with each other in a variety of ways. Some combinations have been found to be beneficial, some to produce negative results. Biodynamic growers try to select suitable combinations of plants for best results.

Sowing by the Moon and Zodiac—biodynamic practitioners follow a sowing chart developed as a result of careful research carried out over many years. It is quite different from popular magazine charts and is not based on folklore or mysticism. By sowing seed according to this chart, a biodynamic gardener/farmer can influence plants to grow more root, leaf, flower or fruit and produce substantially better crops.

Other features of biodynamic practice are available by contacting the Biodynamic Gardeners Association and Biodynamic Resource Centre, PO Box 479, Leongatha VIC 3953, phone number (03) 5664 9219.

B.D.F.G.A.A. (Biodynamic Farmers & Gardeners Association of Australia)
PO Box 54
Bellingen NSW 2454

Bio-dynamics Tasmania
PO Box 177
St Marys 7217 (03) 6372 2211

Organic Federation of Australia
Website: www.ofa.org.au
Canberra Organic Growers Society
www.netspeed.com.au/cogs.htm
Organic Association of Australia
Hotline: 1800 356 299

Cooking Techniques

Cooking without meat, dairy products, fats and a minimum of sugars and salts is to some an enormous challenge. Once you are comfortable with the basic techniques, there is great freedom in eating healthily. Limiting the variety of ingredients that you use in your meals each day enhances freedom too.

One of the major factors in feeling satisfied after eating is to have a good balance of nutrients in your meal and not just vegetables. You can achieve this by having grain in some way with each meal, i.e. porridge at breakfast, bread in some form at lunch and any of the grains made into pasta or in natural form at dinner. Any of the pulses are also good at filling the gap that people using vegetable diets sometimes feel; the need for something more that sends them to the sweets department in the kitchen.

Planning your meal ahead can save you time and money. Apart from shopping time and cost you can save on the fuel costs as well; steam or boil on top of the stove for all your meal or use the oven another time to prepare all the food. Sometimes it can be false economy to precook grains and vegetables. You lose nutrients when reheating food and also expose yourself to bad bacteria. Tests done by government health departments now show that one of the most dangerous things to do with cooked grains and vegetables is to keep them for more than 24 hours. Bacteria can grow even in the fridge. Freezing destroys many nutrients as does the use of microwaves. Microwaves also produce free radicals. For at least six months you need to take all the precautions you can to ensure your body has a chance to rebuild without having to fight the invasion of poisons and toxins. Make sure everything you put in your mouth is helping you to health.

Steaming, dry baking and boiling are the best ways to cook. Use stainless steel, glass or unchipped enamel pots, pans and utensils. Do not use aluminium foil to cover or wrap your food. Covering can be done with a lid or another tray. Store in glass jars or stainless bowls—no plastic if possible. Covering can also be done with greaseproof paper held in place with a string or rubber band. Even a plate on top of a bowl works. One food can contaminate another, particularly cooked and raw food stored together uncovered in the fridge. Greaseproof paper can be used in place of plastic wrap. Also use greaseproof paper to wrap food in small portions if you have to freeze some.

Use a wooden chopping board in preference to a plastic, glass or laminated one. Wood has quite a few advantages. When properly looked after by scrubbing after use, and rinsing off in boiling water, wood will not harbour germs. It is now suggested that plastic boards harbour more bacteria than wooden ones. Wood also saves your very expensive knives from damage. Glass and laminate kill the edges of your knife, so please go to the trouble of looking after your wooden board. It is best to have two or three boards. One for fruit, one for ordinary vegetables and one for the onion–garlic family.

Enjoyment of food and the way you eat is an expression of who you are, regardless of the quality of the food. Enjoyment of good food and company creates such an inner joy that it is possible to taste the sweetest of nectar in even the simplest food. Without this joy, and with no blessing offered, the most wholesome, delicious food can seem tasteless and leave the soul hungry. People who eat for taste and who do not follow a diet or look at nutritional value often develop cravings for something they aren't getting. They bring turmoil into their lives and homes in their constant search, and they eat to satisfy a misplaced hunger. But do not become so rigid or self-righteous about your diet that you annoy others. A bad relationship is more poisonous than grandma's sugar cookies. If you desire such a treat, it is better to have it than to stuff yourself with rice to suppress the desire.

Set aside a special time and place for meals in a clean environment, surrounded with pleasant sounds, aromas, colours, and conversation. Avoid emotionally charged subjects and confused, scattered talk or thoughts. Avoid eating while tired, too hot or too cold, worried, angry, standing, watching TV, reading or before bathing. These activities make the food hard to digest. Relax and get comfortable. Perhaps undertake self-reflection about your condition. Eating is a time to receive offerings in the form of food that nurtures and revitalises your body. Nurture your thoughts as well. Consider your manners insofar as they represent your attitude to others. Give attention to the unique qualities of each food and the work involved in bringing it to you.

Relax after eating, but do not fall asleep or into a stupor. Relaxation helps you digest your food and sleep well at night.

Give thanks before and after eating.

Choose the majority of your foods from local growers. (This helps your health, and your local economy, as well as the environment, by using fewer resources for shipping and refrigeration.) Eat according to your health and constitutional needs.

Liquids and food should not be too hot or too cold. This is especially important for infants and children. Heat debilitates the stomach and creates acidity. Cold paralyses it.

Drinking with meals dilutes the digestive juices. However, a small amount of warm water—four ounces or less—is acceptable. In general, drink water.

Foods and Ingredients

Legumes

Beans, peas and lentils are an important source of protein and are good for the kidneys. Often they are avoided because of problems of flatulence and allergies. The problems may be due to improper preparation and cooking and poor combinations (wrong choice of legume). Legumes such as great northern, navy beans, fava beans, lima, mung beans and chick peas (garbanzo), should be soaked overnight if possible.

Legumes are time consuming but worth the trouble. Preparation and cooking of legumes can be a mystery, but once you get into the routine of using this very important food you will be amazed at the variety you can get in your meals.

Soak them overnight, with a strip of kombu (seaweed) in cold water. Cover them well with water because the beans absorb a lot. Pour off the remaining water when ready to cook as this water has softened the skins and started the sprouting process which eliminates phytic acid and makes more minerals available. Soaking promotes digestibility and faster cooking. Gas-producing enzymes are released into the soak water. After discarding the soak water, add fresh water, and bring legumes to the boil, adding back the kombu. Pour off this second lot of water, cover again with fresh water, add back the kombu, add $\frac{1}{2}$ tsp cumin or fennel for each cup of beans and cook till tender.

Cooking time varies from $\frac{3}{4}$ to $1\frac{1}{2}$ hours, depending on the bean. You can add a little tamari, miso, cider vinegar or a touch of sea salt to the beans when they are almost cooked. Rinse the beans well after cooking. They can be used cold with many varieties of dressings or added to soups or casseroles. Always cook beans separately, then add to other dishes.

See recipes p. 121.

Lentils

Lentils do not require much preparation. Generally it is not necessary to soak lentils, but it does improve their digestibility. If you decide not to soak them, wash them well, removing any small stones or other foreign objects (they often have quite a lot) and cook in plenty of water. They do not expand as much as legumes and only take about thirty minutes to cook. They can be cooked with other foods in the same pot.

Sprouting grains and seeds

Sprouted grain and seeds are at their greatest stage of vitality and have a dramatic increase in vitamin and enzyme content. Protein is turned into amino acids and crude fat is broken down into free fatty acids, making the nutrients easier to assimilate and digest. During cold months, when fresh greens are not readily available, sprouts can be invaluable. Most can be lightly cooked, which provides even better nourishment.

To Sprout

Soak two tablespoons of alfalfa seeds or other legume for at least twelve hours in a wide-mouthed jar. Cover the mouth with muslin or sprouting screen and secure with a rubber band. After soaking, drain and stand upright so excess water drains away. Rinse twice daily until sprouts are ready. Eat when there are two small leaves showing.

Mung bean sprouts—These sprouts have an immune suppressant element when used raw and should always be blanched by plunging into boiling water for a few moments, then rinsed under cold running water before use. This renders the chemical harmless.

Most sprouts from large grains are better cooked lightly.

Alfalfa sprouts—This tiny plant can produce roots up to thirty metres long, thus reaching many minerals and nutrients not reached by other plants. Alfalfa sprouts clean the intestines and take harmful acids out of the blood. They contain ample protein, carotene (equal to carrots), calcium, iron and magnesium. You can see why they are recommended in healthy diets.

Grains

Wheat, barley, rice, millet, buckwheat, oats and corn are all extremely important in a well balanced diet. When prepared properly, they satisfy hunger and taste good. They provide energy and endurance and when combined with legumes and vegetables, supply all the elements of nutrition necessary for human development. They must be chewed properly to incorporate saliva which is needed to start the digestion process.

Soaking in cold water for several hours or overnight if possible, helps to release the nutrients that make grains more easily digested. Do not cook them in the soak water. For those who have poor digestion or are ill, cook the grain in plenty of fresh water till very soft, to almost gruel consistency. This way you gain the most benefit from the grain.

Puffed grains and commercial cereals are highly processed, so limit their use.

BARLEY

Barley is considered the most acid-forming grain but it has so many good properties that they balance out its use. Whole or sproutable barley as against pearl barley contains more fibre, twice the calcium, three times the iron and 25 per cent more protein. Barley is good for the nerves and muscles. It is well worth using whole barley although it does take a little longer to cook. Soaking barley beforehand speeds up cooking time. Cook in the ratio of one cup of barley to four cups of water. Cook for one hour.

Roasting the barley in a dry pan before cooking, just until you can savour the aroma, helps to make barley more alkalising. Soup made with barley and green kale is good for calcium gain.

BRAN

Bran is good for red blood cell formation.

BUCKWHEAT

A strongly flavoured grain, it is called kasha after it has been toasted. Most of the grain is sold this way. Buckwheat has a bioflavinoid called rutin which is considered an antidote against x-rays and radiation. After toasting, buckwheat is an alkalising grain. Make sure you buy hulled buckwheat as it is not possible to cook this grain to an edible state if it is not hulled. Buckwheat sprouts are a good source of enzymes, chlorophyll and vitamins.

CORN

Corn, also called maize, is the most commonly used grain in many countries. Fresh corn on the cob has many enzymes and vitamins. It is best not to cook it for more than a few minutes because cooking makes corn a much more starchy vegetable, and harder to digest. Corn does not contain niacin and should not be a larger part of a diet. It is best in a mixed diet with vegetables.

MILLET

Millet is an alkaline-forming grain which cooks quite quickly. You must use hulled millet. Otherwise you can't cook it soft enough to eat. Millet has a high amino acid and silicon content and can be used frequently by those with candida problems. Cook one cup of millet to three cups of water for about thirty minutes, after which it can be used in the same ways as other grains.

OATS

Oats are rich in silicon and renew bones and connective tissue. They also contain the phosphorus needed by the brain and nerve tissue. Oats also strengthen cardiac muscles; they are generally thought of in the form of breakfast porridge but they can be used in soups, puddings, breads and savoury loaves. For porridge, cook one cup of rolled oats to five cups of water. Stir occasionally till boiling and simmer for 10–15 minutes.

WHEAT

Wheat eaten in small quantities, is one of the most useful grains. It absorbs a wider range of minerals from the soil than other grains. Its nutrient content is similar to that of the human body, so it can be considered the best for human growth and development. Unfortunately, most wheat is over-refined and has been genetically altered to resist diseases since 1926 which partly explains why some people are allergic to it. We are constantly exposed to rancid and over-refined wheat products in the production of food.

SPELT

Spelt is a relative of wheat and not used very much until recently. It has mostly been fed to race horses and cattle as a replacement for oats. Now it has been rediscovered as a beneficial food for humans. Although coming from the wheat family, it can be tolerated by those allergic to wheat, even those with celiac disease. It has a hearty flavour that is lacking in some other grains. Spelt is higher in protein and fat than wheat and its fibre content is water soluble, allowing for better nutrient assimilation by the body. Spelt is a good grain to use for those with digestive problems. It comes in the form of whole grain, pastas, flours, cereals and breads. As it has a very thick husk, spelt is not usually treated with pesticides or other chemicals.

RICE

Whole brown rice has a large amount of B vitamins, bran and fibre, the germ and its essential oils. It is also very easy to digest if cooked and chewed properly. It can be eaten by those who have allergies to gluten. Made into a gruel, rice is very useful when one is very weak and unable to digest most other foods. Rice can have almost any other food added to it, savoury or sweet. Short grain brown rice is the easiest to use. Sprouted rice when used raw in dishes, retains all its nutrients. It loses some of its good properties when cooked.

Rices other than brown have been treated and lost much of their nutrient value. Wild rice is not a true rice, more into the corn family, but makes a nice change for pilaf and rice salads. Brown rice can be cooked by several methods. The most common is one cup of brown rice to three cups of water; cover and bring to the boil; simmer till rice is soft then rinse. According to where the rice was grown, cook for half to three quarters of an hour. Rinse under running hot or cold water, depending on how the rice is to be used.

Breads

See recipes, p. 101.

It is worth making your own bread, as many of the so-called wholesome and healthy wholewheat loaves available in the stores are neither. Often the flour used is mixed wholewheat and processed white so much of the fibre is lost. Even the distinctive brown colouring may come from caramel. Many such loaves often have as many additives as white bread, and are manufactured in much the same way, having no real fermentation time to enhance the flavour.

When making your own bread, choose a hard, stoneground, 100 per cent wholewheat flour. Hard flours, usually made from American or Canadian wheat, have a high gluten content, ensuring a strong, elastic dough which is needed for good results. It is possible to add soft, low-gluten flour like soy for extra flavour and protein, which the dough might otherwise lack.

When making bread use small amounts of sea salt. Sweeteners and oils are not necessary. Make bread in the morning and bake bread at night. On warm sunny days it rises better. Make bread when you feel vital and happy.

Flours

Breads made from freshly milled flour still lose some of their nutrients but these can be regained to a degree by using natural leavening. Sourdough makes a bread into a highly nutritious product. Sourdough bread must be chewed thoroughly and eaten in moderate amounts. Miso, rejuvelac, fermented grains added to sprouted grains are ground up and made into breads (called essene bread) that require no leavening.

Commercial yeasted breads, even wholegrain breads can cause problems. They contain bleach and cause stomach bloat, indigestion and weak intestines. If making your own bread, flours can be mixed together in various proportions. Brown rice flour blends well with other flours and makes a smooth bread. Buckwheat must be used with wheat or rice flour. Millet must be combined with wheat flour. Mix a third to two-thirds wheat. Cornmeal is better mixed with small amounts of other flours. Soy flour has to be added to other flours in small amounts. If the flour is freshly ground and has some oil content, it is best to keep it in a covered container in the refrigerator. Rising agents added to flour labelled as 'self raising flour', are not healthy. There are several good alternatives to the usual baking powder available. A substitute for baking powder available from health food stores is sometimes called Pritikin baking powder. Any similar product from a health food store is acceptable.

Barley flour makes a sticky bread and can be combined 50:50 with wholewheat flour for lightness.

Brown rice yields a sweeter and smoother bread. Blends well with other flours. Use flour 20 per cent in combination.

Buckwheat makes a good dark and heavy winter bread. Use in combinations with wheat and rice flours.

Chestnut flour gives a light bread; good combined with small amounts of other flours.

Corn meal flour gives a good light bread; best combined with small amounts of other flours.

Garbanzo (chick pea) flour can be used alone or mixed with other flours; especially good in sauces and pancakes.

Kamut flour is light in texture and can be substituted in equal amounts for wholewheat pastry flour in cake, pie and muffin recipes.

Millet flour always combine with other flours, especially whole wheat (one-third millet to two-thirds wholewheat).

Oat flour is light in texture and can be substituted for pastry flour. It adds moistness to cakes and pastries; add approximately 20 per cent to corn, wholewheat or rice flours.

Rye flour makes a sticky bread and can be combined 50:50 with rice or wholewheat flour for a lighter bread; 100 per cent rye bread greatly improves in flavour after several days.

Soy flour Add small amounts to other flours for a smoother and moister texture.

Spelt flour can be substituted 100 per cent for wheat in bread recipes; usually well tolerated by those allergic to wheat.

Pastas

See recipes p. 113.

There is a large variety of pastas on the market, made from almost every grain. Because some grains are inclined to be more acid forming that others, it is best to use all the different ones available. Those made from wheat are the most acid forming and as all pastas are processed, keep your consumption reasonably low, balancing out your meal with fresh ingredients in the form of vegetable sauce or a salad.

Care needs to be taken with the cooking of rice and buckwheat-based pastas as it is easy to overcook them. A good rule of thumb for most pastas is to cook them 'al dente' in plenty of boiling water. Drain and rinse under cold running water and plunge back into a pot of fresh boiling water for a few minutes just before serving.

Seaweeds

The powers of sea vegetables have been known for centuries. Sea plants contain ten to twenty times the minerals of land plants, and an abundance of vitamins and other properties essential to man. Certain ones actually remove radioactive and toxic metal wastes from our bodies. They can remove phlegm and clean the lymphatic system. They alkalise the blood, lower cholesterol and fat in the blood, and are beneficial to the thyroid gland. They are excellent sources of calcium, amino acids and iron, varying from ten times to three thousand times, depending on the type of sea vegetable. They don't absorb toxins; rather they transform toxic metals to harmless salts which the body can excrete through the intestines. All sea vegetables are invaluable for regaining health and keeping it. There is also a product called Float Leaf coming from Tasmania now. This is also kelp. Easily obtainable sea vegetables are:

Agar agar or Kanten

A vegetable gelatin, apart from its setting properties, agar agar does not need refrigeration to set to a firm jelly. It promotes digestion and contains no calories, but has most of the properties of other seaweeds although not quite as high. To use agar, add one dessertspoon to a cup of hot liquid, stir and simmer till dissolved. Add to juice to make a jelly or to cooked vegetables to make a terrine or aspic-based mould.

Hijiki and arame

These are thread-like lengths of seaweed containing vitamin B2 and niacin. As well as the other nutrients, they support hormone function. Soak for thirty minutes in warm water and chop; there is no need to cook them, add them to any grain, soup, bread, salad, tofu or vegetable dish.

Kombu and kelp

These greatly increase the nutritional value of any food prepared with them as they are considered the most completely mineralised food. Kelp is available in powder or tablet form. It can be used in a salt shaker on the table and because of its salty flavour can replace the need for salt in foods. Kombu and kelp are excellent added to dried beans during cooking. The minerals help to balance the protein and oils and increase the digestibility of beans by breaking down the tough fibres. Break or cut the kombu with scissors, add to soup, salads or bean dishes. If using in salads, cook for one hour first. For soups or bean dishes, just add kombu with other ingredients.

Nori

Its fibres are more tender than most seaweeds. They have the highest protein content and are the most easily digested of the seaweed family. Rich in vitamin A, B and niacin, nori is good for goitre and high blood pressure, as well as containing all the other properties and uses of seaweeds. Nori comes in sheets and can be used as is. It is best to buy toasted nori because it is more tender. It can be used in sushi, crumbled over any food, hot or cold or in sandwiches, dressings or spreads.

Beneficial Additions

CHLOROPHYLL
The blood of plants, chlorophyll in plants gives them their green colour. When compared to a molecule of haemoglobin, the oxygen carrier in human blood, chlorophyll is almost identical. By taking a dash of chlorophyll in some form each day you can add vital nutrients, minerals, enzymes, oxygen and protein to your blood. Eating green leafy plants, or taking 'green' powders if fresh greens are not available, is very important.

BIOSTRATH
This food supplement consists of natural substances. The manufacturing process does not destroy the active ingredients. Developing this product has taken ten years, and the assessment of its usefulness in increasing the resistance of the body to disease was done by independent specialists.

LACTOBACILLUS BULGARICUS
All types of yoghurt and fermented dairy and soy products have a very beneficial effect on our system. *Lactobacillus* is particularly important after taking antibiotics, as many of the good bacteria or flora in the bowel are destroyed by antibiotics. Yoghurt and similar fresh products and *Lactobacillus* tablets restore good bacteria, thus alleviating many lower intestinal problems in young and old alike. Be aware that not all commercial yoghurts have a good ratio of *Lactobacillus*. Read the labels carefully and use the pure product, not those with added fruits and flavours.

NUTRITIONAL YEAST
Nutritional yeast is marketed under the name of Red Star. This product can be useful as an additional source of B vitamins, folic acid and many minerals and provides a small amount of vitamin B12. This yeast product can be used to add flavour to many dishes. Add it to juices, cereals or smoothies, gravies, sauces, soups and salads. This type of yeast can be tolerated by those with candida problems.

Soy products

MISO
Miso is a fermented paste made from soy beans, grains and mould (koji). There are three basic types of miso—soybean

(hatcho); barley (mugi); rice (kome), as well as many variations. Miso contains amino acids, protein, traces of vitamin B12 and is a live food containing lactobacillus bacteria. It creates an alkaline condition in the body that promotes resistance to disease. Most of the nutrients in miso are destroyed by boiling, so add the paste to soups and stews just before serving. A teaspoon of miso dissolved in a cup of hot water has the ability to settle an upset stomach by creating an alkaline environment. It helps too when you have overeaten or undergoing chemotherapy. Because it adds a hearty flavour, miso is sometimes overused by people when changing to a meatless diet. Be aware that it is stronger than meat because of its ageing and sea salt content. When used moderately, it provides excellent nutrition. You can add it to stews, soups, gravies, sauces, dressings, stuffings, dips and spread sparingly on toast.

Soy Milk

There are many soy milks on the market. Choose one that is made from organic whole soy beans. Use it in moderation. This will provide protein and calcium and can be used in the same way as cow's milk (except for small children). There are oat milk and rice milk as well. These products are good to use as they do not have the digestion problems that can arise from using cow's milk.

Soy beans

They are very alkalising and can be a valuable food. They help remove toxins from the body and provide phyto-oestrogens and tryptophan. Soy beans are the hardest bean to digest. Unless very well cooked they inhibit digestive enzymes. The fermentation process such as used in the making of tempeh, tofu, miso and soy sauce eliminates the trypsin effect of the soy bean.

Tofu

This is a processed soy bean curd that originated in China thousands of years ago to improve the digestibility of the valued soy bean. Tofu contains protein, B vitamins and minerals, and a calcium content equal to that of cow's milk. We do not need a lot of tofu. Tofu made with magnesium chloride salt should be avoided. Tofu is a very versatile product; it can be baked, steamed, boiled, sauted and even eaten raw. Because of its blandness it soaks up whatever flavouring is put with it. Store and keep in a cool place covered with water, in an airtight container or sealed jar. Change the water daily.

Tempeh

From Indonesia, this fermented food is made from cooked soy beans bound together by a mould. There are many flavours and varieties. Asian tempeh can be a good source of vitamin B12 but when made in Western countries, the

B12 content is not as high because of the clean environment of the manufacturing area so B12 is often injected into the finished product. Tempeh must be cooked either by baking, steaming or boiling. It is improved by marinating, as is tofu.

Soy Yoghurt

This has the same nutritional properties as cow's milk yoghurt, while having the added benefits of the soy bean.

Herbs

Fresh herbs have many benefits in gaining and maintaining health. They contain valuable oils, minerals, trace elements and many other important substances which give herbs their distinctive flavour and uses. They should never be used individually to excess as they can have a very strong therapeutic effect. To use the right herbs for healing you should seek the advice of a health professional. If you have a distinct preference for one to the exclusion of others, check with a naturopath that it is OK for you.

Fresh herbs are not as strong as dried. Generally you need twice as much of a fresh herb as you do dried. The flavour of dried herbs can be similar to fresh but the therapeutic effect is lessened.

Growing and then drying your herbs can be a rewarding experience. There are many books to advise you about growing and drying but this process can be very simple. Cut and spread your herbs out on a flat surface and dry in the shade or tie in bundles and hang up so the air can circulate through them.

Herb teas can also be therapeutic. Don't drink one to the exclusion of all others or you may have a reaction.

(See more about herbal teas under beverages, p. 52).

Basil

An excellent flavouring for stocks and soups and tomato dishes, basil is thought to help the brain function and clear the head. Being a strong herb it is classed as having allspice qualities.

Bay leaves

Bay leaf is an important part of the bouquet garni and is especially good in vegetable soups. The only one of this herb family that is used in cooking. The valuable oil is very aromatic, a little bitter and it stimulates the appetite.

Bowles mint

Grows in most gardens and pots and is used with many foods. It can be added to beans, peas, potatoes, carrots and sauces. Goes well in lentil soup and hot or cold drinks.

Celery leaves

The leaves are classed as a herb as are the seeds. Celery has many vitamins and mineral salts and has an effect on the whole glandular system. It also stimulates the digestion. Celery is a good flavouring to use for people with diabetes.

CHIVES

The smallest of the onion family, they are rich in flavour and do not upset the digestive system as onions can do. Chives can be generously used in most dishes, raw or cooked and are easy to grow.

CORIANDER

The fresh leaves impart a very distinctive flavour to foods. It is classed as an appetiser and in small quantities has a calming effect on the system. Used mostly in soups and casseroles and with pulses. Used a lot in Indian cooking.

DANDELION

Is a very nutritious herb and should be used frequently, particularly in spring as dandelion is a good source of minerals and vitamins. Dandelion added to salad in spring is very good for you.

DILL

Its very distinctive flavour makes it most frequently used in pickling cucumbers. This process makes the cucumber more digestible. Dill leaf and seeds enhance bland vegetables and go well in sauces. Dill has laxative qualities too. It is used in gripe water for babies. Dill strongly resembles fennel in appearance but not in flavour.

FENNEL

Known for its ability to help you digest oily fish, it is also very good for the eyes and skin. Helps to alleviate flatulence and is useful in a weight loss program.

GARLIC

The most common of kitchen herbs, along with parsley. Unlike parsley, garlic has a very strong taste and aroma. Like many herbs it stimulates the digestion, and can remove catarrh from the intestinal tract and relieves all intestinal infections. Helps the gall bladder and liver and is generally regarded as good for our health.

GINGER

Fresh green ginger made into tea is good for colds and fevers. Grated, it adds flavour and digestive qualilties to many dishes, savoury and sweet. Ginger helps relieve the flatulence that sometimes accompanies the eating of legumes. A small amount of ginger juice added to vegetable juices makes a pleasant change. Ginger helps alleviate nausea and vomiting.

HORSERADISH

The root from this plant has a delicious hot pungency. It has anti-colic qualities and in fact has substances which kill bacteria. It is useful for keeping the intestinal tract in good condition. It stimulates the appetite and helps the liver function.

Lemon balm

Sometimes considered a weed, but it has many virtues. It has anti-spasmodic qualities and stimulates the heart, yet has a calming effect on the nervous system. This herb makes a delicious hot drink and the leaves can be used in salads, pasta sauces, desserts and in fruit drinks.

Marjoram

A strong spicy herb, mainly used with meat but can add flavour to vegetable soups and casseroles. It is especially useful in vegetable stuffing and for potatoes and all pulses.

Nasturtium

Almost all of this plant can be eaten—the flower in salads, the chopped leaves in sandwiches and the seeds as mock capers. Also nasturtium has a very high vitamin C content and is considered a type of herbal penicillin. Care should be taken with its use as the leaves have a very strong peppery flavour and left too long with other foods can leave them bitter.

Parsley

Goes with almost any dish and is the most useful herb for the kitchen. It contains many vitamins and minerals and all parts of the plant can be used. Parsley emphasises the flavour of foods without adding a strong accent. It masks the odour of strong vegetables like onions and carrots. It can be used in moderate quantities, even juiced to add to vegetable juice nutrition.

Peppermint

Mostly used for a tea which is known to settle tummy upsets and it is not generally used in cooking (see Beverages, p. 54).

Sage

A flowering herb that needs to be used carefully as it can overpower foods. It does not seem to have any great health-giving properties. Sage can be used with all pulses and spinach, onions, beans and beetroot. It also adds a pleasant flavour to cold fruit drinks.

Thyme

The strongest flavoured of all herbs—a little goes a long way. It is classed as a digestive, particularly needed with fatty foods. It has strong antibiotic qualities. Thyme can be used in thick soups, with beans and all fungi, in tomato-based sauces and minestrone soup. Lemon thyme has a more delicate flavour and is generally used in desserts and drinks.

Sweeteners

Sugar

A major force in our bodies, we need sugar, but in the right form. The sugars in whole foods are balanced with the proper minerals. The energy obtained from the breaking down of these sugars is enduring.

The highs and lows we experience from taking in refined sugars cause among many other conditions, an acid effect in the body. This leads to a blood sugar imbalance and more sugar cravings, as well as an increase in the craving for meat and other high protein foods. There are better sources of sugar than the white crystals so commonly used. Whole vegetable foods chewed very well will gradually reduce the cravings for sweetness from the wrong sources.

HONEY

In small quantities honey can be substituted for sugar. But honey is highly refined by the bees and has more calories than white sugar. Raw honey does contain some minerals and enzymes and does not upset the body's mineral balance.

GRAIN MALTS

Made from fermented rice and barley, these malts are only one-third as sweet as sugar yet they contain complex sugars and many of the nutrients in grains. They take longer to digest so they don't produce the highs and lows that one can experience when eating cane sugar.

STEVIA POWDER OR LIQUID

Becoming better known, it is a small herb that is native to Latin America and the southern United States. The leaves and flowers of this plant are thirty times sweeter than sugar. Stevia can be used without ill effect by diabetics. Stevia does not work as well as other sweeteners in baked goods.

Fruit concentrates

Another source of sweetening, but because of their concentrated nature, their sugar content becomes very high. They are far from being whole unprocessed foods. Use with caution as sugars of most kinds deplete the minerals in our bodies and we can't afford that depletion. Sugars also lower the immune system. Dried fruits which have been soaked well in water can be pureed and used as sweeteners.

Cane Sugar Substitutes

Not all recipes will work with sugar substitutes. 1 cup of white or brown sugar is equivalent to:

- $3/4$ cup pure maple syrup. Reduce total liquids by 2 tablespoons.
- $1/2$ cup honey. Reduce total liquids by $1/4$ cup.
- 1 cup molasses. Reduce total liquids by $1/2$ cup.
- $1 1/2$ cups sorghum. Reduce total liquids by $1/4$ cup.

- 1 cup pure corn syrup. Reduce total liquid by ¼ cup.
- When using substitutes, prevent over-browning by lowering the baking temperature by 20°C (40°F).
- To measure liquid sweeteners, first moisten cup with hot water or oil.
- Use unsweetened fruit juice in place of other liquid.
- When using carob powder rather than chocolate use a little less sweetening than the recipe calls for as carob is a natural sweetener. Substitute carob for chocolate on a 1:1 basis. One square of cooking chocolate is equivalent to 1 tablespoon of carob powder and ½ table-spoon margarine or 2 tablespoons water.
- When substituting glucose or dextrose for sugar, remember they are usually derived from corn.
- Fructose (fruit sugar) can be used to replace sugar in cereals, drinks and desserts. Be careful you are not allergic to the fruit from which the sugar is derived.
- In baking, use dried fruits to add sweetness.

Eggs

Eggs have numerous functions in baked products and it is not possible to replace all these with substitutes. They act as a structural component and nutrient source. They provide lightness, flavour and moisture. Structure is not severely affected by omitting eggs as long as a binder and sufficient liquid is added (3 tablespoons liquid for every egg omitted). The nutrient quality in eggs cannot be substituted. Lecithin in egg yolk acts as an emulsifier for the fat in baked foods. In egg-free recipes the fat is often melted and boiled with the liquid and quickly stirred into the dry ingredients to effect dispersion of the fat and water parts.

For one egg, substitute:
- 2 tablespoons cold cooked sago (only successful for substituting up to 2 eggs).
- 2 tablespoons flour, ½ teaspoon seasoning, ½ teaspoon baking powder, and 2 tablespoons liquid.
- 2 tablespoons water, ½ teaspoon baking powder. This is good in biscuit and cake recipes requiring only 1 egg.
- 1 mashed banana in biscuits, cakes, pancakes and muffins.
- Gelatine works well in puddings and desserts; 1 tablespoon to every 2 cups of liquid.
- Soak 250 g dried apricots in water for several hours or overnight. Blend, add extra water if necessary, strain and store in the refrigerator. One generous table-spoon will substitute for 1 egg. (Freeze portions for further use.)
- Flaxseed is a good egg substitute in biscuit, cake, pancake and muffin recipes. Add 1 cup ground flaxseed to 3 cups cold water. Bring to the boil, stirring constantly. Boil for 3 minutes. Cool. Store in the refrigerator in a closed jar.

One egg is equivalent to 1 tablespoon of flaxseed mixture.

● Replace egg as the binder in meat loaf or rissoles with 1 cup puffed rice to each 500 g mince.

● Use tapioca, or arrowroot flour as binders. Instead of using 2 cups rice flour, use 1½ cups rice flour and ½ cup tapioca or arrowroot flour and 2 teaspoons extra liquid.

Handy Hints

● In eggless mixtures, beat more between the addition of new ingredients and bake immediately the beating is completed to prevent the escape of air.

● If the recipe is egg-free, milk-free and gluten-free, bake at a lower temperature for longer.

Salt

Most of our vegetables are grown in demineralised soil, thus one feels there is something missing in taste when we eat them. Instinct has us reaching for the salt which we seem to feel is what is lacking. Some vegetables have a natural salty taste i.e. sea vegetables, that is because they have a high mineral content. We feel the need for minerals is satisfied by adding salt.

Natural occurring 'salts' found in wholefoods have an alkalising effect on the blood i.e. miso, and as the body has to have its acid v alkaline ratio in balance we do need some salt. Processed salt does not have a beneficial effect on the blood.

Carob

The carob tree is one of the oldest known fruit-bearing trees. It originated in the Mediterranean region and was known as St John's bread. Carob flour and powder supply protein, carbohydrates, minerals, calcium and phosphorus. Carob has a very low fat content. It can be used as a substitute for chocolate or coffee in cooked products and can be used in hot or cold drinks. It needs no added sweeteners. Carob is an alkaline-forming food and does not contain caffeine.

Oils

Omega 3 in particular, is found in fish oil and the flax plant. It has been proven that a diet with adequate amounts of this and other essential fatty acids goes a long way in assisting the return of health. Modern diets are deficient in essential fatty acids. Flax seed and its freshly pressed oil may be one of the best specific remedies because it contains these essential fatty acids—alpha-linolenic acid (Omega 3) and non-rancid linolenic acid.

Several diets devised by leading experts encourage the use of cold-extracted flax oil. (Healing properties of flax are destroyed when the oil is heated.) Flax oil can be taken by itself or mixed in juices, salad dressings, spreads or poured directly on to vegetables after serving.

Essential fatty acids are converted into prostaglandins in the body. Prostaglandins are thought to play a role in the regulation and function of every organ and cell in the body.

Oils are required for the proper function of the immune system. Beneficial oils increase cell proliferation and normalise malignant and mutated cells, thereby promoting cancer reversal and the reversal of many other diseases including heart and vascular problems.

Any cold extracted oils are good. If heat is used in the production of oils it renders them useless for a health-promoting diet.

Seasoning

Seasoning food can be a problem when the usual condiments are forbidden. Liquid bouillons and dried organic vegetable powders can provide added flavour in your soups, sauces and casseroles. Miso, tamari and soy are useful as are fresh herbs and spices. (See herbs, p. 39.) Natural yeast powders can also help with flavour while adding extra nutrients. This type of yeast does not have the same effect in the body as baker's yeast i.e. candida problems.

Vegetables

Vegetables cleanse the body and purify the blood. Lightly cooked vegetables retain most of their vitality. Long, slow cooking improves digestibility. See recipes, p. 114.

ASPARAGUS
A good tonic for the kidneys. Break off the tough stem and discard and boil the rest for 7–8 minutes.

BEETROOT
Good for liver ailments. It improves circulation and purifies the blood. Boil whole and serve hot or cold. To serve raw, scrub and grate, adding a little dressing. Beetroots are 'eliminating' foods.

BROCCOLI
Contains vitamins A and B5 and has more vitamin C than citrus. It also contains sulphur and iron. If cooked lightly, broccoli will retain all its chlorophyll content which reduces its gas-forming properties. Can be used hot, or cold in salads.

CABBAGE
Benefits all stomach problems. Helps get rid of constipation. Has more vitamin C than oranges. There is 40 per cent more calcium in green cabbage than white cabbage. Has good sulphur content and is good for purifying the blood. Contains iodine and vitamin E and calcium. Steam, boil or serve cold—shredded into coleslaw or other salads.

CARROTS
Alkaline forming which helps to clear acidic blood conditions. Carrots are one of the richest sources of pro-vitamin A, an anti-oxidant that protects against cancer. Carrots stimulate the release of wastes. They can dissolve tumours and growths and clear the intestinal tract. They can be boiled, baked, steamed or eaten raw.

CELERY
Improves digestion and liver function. It reduces acids in the body and adds sodium. Celery is the highest source of sodium in vegetables, and a few stalks eaten raw will satisfy salt cravings. High

in silicon, celery helps to renew bones and arteries and all connective tissue. Good for high blood pressure. It can be used raw or cooked.

CUCUMBER

Counteracts toxins and cleanses the blood. It reduces acids in the body and adds sodium. Acts as a digestive aid and cools in summer. Juice is good for kidney and bladder problems. Contains an enzyme, erepsin that breaks down protein and cleanses the intestines. Use raw or cooked.

GARLIC

Very useful for promoting circulation and eliminating unfavourable bacteria in yeasts. It improves healthy bacteria in the intestines and eliminates many toxins from the body, just to name a few attributes. (See also onions.)

LETTUCE

Leafy lettuce is much richer than head lettuce. It contains chlorophyll in the outer green leaves, also iron and vitamins A and C. Do not use hydroponically grown lettuce or other produce grown this way, as the chemicals used to grow them are concentrated in the recycled water. Even if it is natural fertilisation it can become too concentrated.

MUSHROOMS

Even ordinary button mushrooms have antibiotic properties; they increase immunity against disease and increase appetite while decreasing fat levels in blood and reduce mucus in the respiratory tract.

Shiitake

These mushrooms look more like toadstools. They can be obtained fresh sometimes but are available in dried form from some health food shops and all Asian grocery stores. This little mushroom has a chemical called lentinen in it which has been shown to be an immune system enhancer, along with being a good source of germanium, an element that improves cellular oxygenation and also enhances immunity.

Fresh shiitake can be used the same way as button mushrooms, but the tough little stalk needs to be removed and discarded. Dried shiitake need to be soaked for at least thirty minutes in warm water before being used in the same way as button mushrooms.

OLIVES

The highest source of potassium. Black being better generally.

ONIONS

The onion family (chives, leeks, garlic, onion) all share similar properties. They are rich in sulphur which purifies the body and clean the arteries, and help remove heavy metals and avoid clotting. (See also garlic.)

PARSNIP

Good for the spleen and pancreas; helps avoid blood clotting and benefits the stomach, liver and gall bladder. Best used cooked in soups and stews.

PUMPKIN

Helps regulate blood sugar levels and can help bronchial problems. Best used cooked—boil, bake, steam, mash or use in casseroles and stews.

RADISHES

Good for detoxing the body. They cut mucus and help prevent viral infection.

SPINACH AND SILVER BEET

Rich in iron and chlorophyll, they also have oxalic acid, so not too much of them. Their vitamin A is useful. Wash carefully and steam or boil. Small amounts can be eaten raw.

SWEET POTATO AND YAMS

Rich in vitamin A and remove toxins from the body. Good mixed with pumpkin in a soup or sliced and baked in the oven. Add some garlic and a little water.

Fruit

We are conditioned from an early age to eat lots of fruit. But generally as far as health is concerned we should eat only those fruits that grow naturally in a season, and which grow close to where we live. A lot of fruit is picked before it is properly ripe. As such it does not contain the nutrients we expect. Heavy spraying of fruit does not allow it to be alkalising as fruit should be, and the chemicals concentrate in the juice. Drinking a lot of sweet fruit juice can be very weakening and may promote the growth of yeasts in the body. Apples and dried fruits are not so bad in this category.

Fruit is generally considered not to mix well with other food in regard to digestion. Fruits digest fast and start to ferment in the stomach while waiting for the rest of the food to be processed. It is better to have a fruit meal on an empty stomach, i.e. breakfast or mid-afternoon and eat whole fruits rather than juices. Anyone with deficiency conditions should avoid raw fruit. Fruit juices should only be drunk four hours after a meal or one hour before a meal.

APPLES

One of the most useful fruits, they contain pectin, which helps remove residues of radiation and toxic metal and helps clear cholesterol. The malic acid in apples clears harmful bacteria in the digestive tract. Apples and their juice are beneficial for the liver and gall bladder.

APRICOTS

Can be useful for those with anaemia. Apricots are high in cobalt and copper and are useful too for problems with lungs such as asthma. If you tend to have trouble with diarrhoea, limit apricots in your diet.

AVOCADO

A natural souce of lecithin and mono-saturated fats or oil. A good protein and lecithin source and rich in copper, which helps to build red blood cells.

BANANAS

Good for reducing blood pressure, and because of their high potassium content also good for treating hypertension.

Steamed bananas are good for diarrhoea, colitis and piles.

CHERRIES

High in easily assimilated iron and good for gout and arthritis, they help eliminate excess body acid. Try to obtain organic cherries as most commercially grown ones are very heavily sprayed.

FIGS

One of the most alkalising fruits and can help balance acid conditions resulting from a diet high in meat and refined food. They have a good source of sodium. Good for cleansing the bowel when constipation is a problem.

GRAPEFRUIT

Similar properties to lemons but are not as useful.

GRAPES

Red ones particularly are good blood builders and improve the cleansing function of our glands. Good to eat when there is a problem with liver such as hepatitis and jaundice. The juice improves kidney function. Chew grape seeds to remove catarrh and mucus.

LEMONS

All citrus fruits have a content of vitamin C and also help with digestion. Lemons are particularly cleansing. The juice in a little water first thing in the morning helps to destroy bad bacteria in the mouth and intestines and encourages the production of bile by improving liver function. Best fruit if you overeat fat and protein. Lemon cleans the blood and helps the circulation; benefits liver and absorption of minerals; reduces flatulence and calms the nerves.

MULBERRIES

Have a tonic effect on the kidneys, liver and blood.

ORANGES

Usually sprayed very heavily and picked while still green and can be quite acidic. Best eaten as a whole fruit and not as a juice.

PAWPAW

Particularly good for treating indigestion; good if you have eaten too much protein.

PEARS

Can be very beneficial when problems arise with constipation. Eat whole or have the juice first thing in the morning. Pears also help to cleanse the lungs of mucus.

PINEAPPLE

Should be very ripe when eaten and can then help to increase digestive ability because of its enzyme bromelin.

PLUMS

Red ones particularly are useful with all liver problems.

POMEGRANATE

Thought to be beneficial in the treatment of some types of cancer.

PRUNES

Have the highest content of nerve salts.

RASPBERRIES

Thought to be beneficial in the treatment of some types of cancer.

STRAWBERRIES

Good to eat a while before a meal as they can stimulate the appetite. They are rich in silicon and are good as a spring cleanser. Organic please as they and cherries are the most highly sprayed fruits. Strawberries are good for the spleen and pancreas; they help abdominal pain and swelling.

Beverages

Plain water is very necessary to life and we should drink as much of it as we can. But we can make some of it more interesting and therapeutic by adding various herbs. There are a huge number of herb teas on the market but you should avoid drinking one or two of them exclusively. Check with a natural therapist before using a particular one on a regular basis. Vary them for the properties they contain. This is a short description of a few of the many herb teas available and most commonly used. Experiment a bit and also consult a qualified person to guide you with the therapeutic use of these teas. (See also herbs, p. 39.)

BUTTERMILK
Is good as a bowel laxative.

GOAT'S MILK
Fresh or in dried whey supplies potassium, sodium phosphate and calcium.

ALFALFA TEA
One of the best teas to drink when changing from a meat-based diet to using more carbohydrates, as it helps to balance out the acid produced by the stomach for protein digestion. This very deep-rooted plant also contains many minerals and vitamins not usually available from other plant sources. Combining mint with alfalfa helps the digestion even more.

ANISEED TEA
The aniseed flavour is enjoyed by most people including children. Aniseed works within the pancreas, helping the digestive process. It is very useful when one has catarrhal, head and breathing problems.

APPLE CIDER VINEGAR
Cider vinegar should be organic, naturally brewed, unfiltered and unpasteurised. It can reduce accumulations in the liver and abdomen while we are in the transition period of changing from a meat based diet to a vegetable diet. Cider vinegar can provide relief while toxins are being released.

BOUILLON

One teaspoon of mineral bouillon in a cup of hot water is a tasty hot drink instead of soup.

CHAMOMILE TEA

This is a very gentle and useful tea as it has calming qualities for both children and adults. The tea can also settle an upset stomach, quieten the thoughts after a busy day and relieve cramping spasms suffered by some women. If you have a cup of chamomile tea a while before your meal it will help your stomach prepare to digest your food. This is one of the herb teas that can safely be used frequently by all ages. A weak solution in a bath also helps relieve the pain of sunburn.

COMFREY TEA

While not a generally well known tea it can be useful after surgery of any kind and when bones are broken. It helps with cell regeneration and the growth of new tissue. Comfrey tea needs some help with flavour so you can add a mint or some other strongly flavoured tea to it. Comfrey helps to neutralise uric acid conditions like gout and arthritis. Comfrey taken to excess can be dangerous.

DANDELION ROOT GROUNDS

One of the most useful beverages in a tea or coffee form (which is the most commonly used). Dandelion contains many substances, iron and calcium, choline (helps with cholesterol) vitamins A and D. The bitterness stimulates the gall bladder, and helps control viruses like hepatitis. Dandelion tea removes poisons from the body and is a blood cleanser. Because of its therapeutic and digestive qualities, it's also helpful to the gall bladder and liver. The roots are used to make a coffee substitute.

Dandelion 'coffee' made from dried roasted roots, not the instant product, can be valuable and a good substitute in flavour for ordinary coffee. To make the coffee place three tablespoons of the roasted root in one litre of water, bring to the boil and simmer for several minutes. Strain off the liquid to drink, returning any liquid not used to the granules, put in a covered container and refrigerate till next time required. Then add a little more water and bring to the boil again. This process can be done three to four times. You can add a little honey and soy milk if liked to the coffee when serving. Two to three cups a day is a good tonic for the liver. (See also herbs, p. 40.)

FLAX SEED TEA

This tea can be made from crushed whole brown seeds. It can be particularly useful as a laxative tea as the seed contains 30–40 per cent oil and some protein, phosphorus and lecithin. This is also useful for inflammation in the kidneys and bladder and the whole digestive tract.

FENNEL TEA

Fennel has an aniseed flavour and is very pleasant to drink. It has many uses, one of which is helping the pancreas to metabolise fats and sugars. It can certainly help your body cope with a diet that consists of take-away and instant foods. It can help you to lose a little weight caused by over-consumption of fats and sugars. Along the way it can take away the craving for these foods.

GINGER TEA

Ginger tea can step up the hydrochloric acid needed to digest food properly. It also helps to get rid of wind if you eat too fast or improperly. Ginger tea makes one feel a whole lot more comfortable by stimulating saliva and settling down the digestive tract.

LEMON TEA

Used as a booster in a lot of herb teas and as a cooling drink. Its flavour is acceptable to most. The lemon can balance the minerals and choline and is a mild digestive aid. It cools and clears the head as well.

PEPPERMINT TEA

The most common of the mint teas, peppermint has a refreshing action in summer and warming in winter. It settles overloaded, windy stomachs and clears stuffy sinuses and heads. Combined with alfalfa it is invaluable as an after-dinner drink.

RED CLOVER TEA

This is a blood tonic because of its high content of iron and copper salts. It cleans the blood and improves haemoglobin levels. This is a powerful herb, particularly useful for cleansing the female reproductive systems over a couple of weeks. It should not be taken on a regular basis.

ROSEHIP TEA

A good pick-me-up tea, it can be drunk during the day. But it is not good at night because of its stimulating qualities. In winter, have it hot with lemon and a pinch of cinnamon. In summer try it cold with peppermint and ice. Rosehip tea is full of vitamin C, P and K, iron and copper. It helps with viscosity of the blood and varicose vein problems. It can replace coffee as a stimulant.

VALERIAN TEA

Although this rather unusual flavoured tea is not easily drunk, it is one of the most therapeutic of herb teas. As a natural sedative it cannot be beaten. It is not habit forming. Before bed valerian tea relaxes spasms and cramps. The calcium relaxes internal organs and potassium phosphate relaxes nerves, promoting sleep from which you awaken really refreshed. This is a medicinal tea and care should be taken using it.

JUICES

CLOCKWISE FROM LEFT: Carrot and celery; beetroot, celery and carrot; carrot; green leaf and lemon (page 55)

Breakfast choices

Top row from left: Fresh fruit, yoghurt oil mix (page 62), dandelion coffee (page 63), honey, soy milk

Middle row from left: Sultanas, stewed pears, muesli, porridge (page 63)

Bottom row from left: Almonds, fruit toast, linseeds

TOP LEFT: Lunch — Miso soup (page 64)

BOTTOM RIGHT: Dinner — Legume burgers (page 65)

FROM LEFT: Lunch – Grilled vegetables in focaccia (page 66)

BOTTOM RIGHT: Dinner – Mushroom soup (page 66)

TOP RIGHT: Dinner – Spaghetti with golden sauce (page 67)

Juices

Raw juices are rich in vitamins, minerals, trace elements and enzymes. These very necessary elements are easily assimilated into the bloodstream without putting more strain on the digestive system, which is always under stress when we are ill. The nutritive elements in juices are beneficial in normalising body processes. They supply much needed elements to activate all regeneration. Juices of vegetables have an alkalising effect on the blood helping to bring the pH back to the right acid-alkaline balance.

Mineral imbalance in the tissues is one of the causes of lack of oxygen in the body, which can lead to disease. Raw juices help our bodies to expel toxins by breaking down and disposing of old and dying cells, then revitalising the active cells, leading to the building of new healthy cells.

Juices should be consumed slowly, sipping and mixing the juice with the saliva in the mouth. Maximum benefit comes by drinking the juice within ten minutes of its preparation, and taking ten minutes to drink a glass. Try not to use more than four vegetables in a juice and do not mix fruit and vegetable juices together. Diarrhoea sometimes results when you take a number of fresh juices, as long as it is not too severe, don't be concerned. This is nature doing a little house cleaning. Possibly, you will lose a little weight, but this will be regained in time by the rebuilding of your body.

Mixed together in a juice, fruit and vegetables can cause a few digestive 'experiences'. Fruits digest faster than vegetables, and then they have to wait around for the vegies to be processed. In that time, they start to ferment and can cause gas problems.

Carrots can be mixed with most other vegetables and are one of the most used juices. Carrots with celery and parsley—use 70 per cent carrot. Carrots with beetroot, use 80 per cent carrot. Carrots with parsley and garlic use 98 per cent carrot.

A juice made of fresh green leaves is full of chlorophyll. The great bowel cleanser. A dirty bowel gives rise to dirty blood. The outer dark green leaves of lettuce, a few spinach or silverbeet leaves, some cabbage leaves and a little celery or green capsicum will make a great cleansing juice. You can add a spoonful or two of a powdered green supplement, if you wish to make a more potent juice. The green powders are quite beneficial and can be used in water on their own if it's not convenient for you to make a fresh green juice.

Certain cancer diets recommend over twelve juices per day but at the Centre we serve on average six. One of the reasons for this is time. Unless there is someone with you who has a lot of time to help with your food shopping and preparation, it can be very exhausting trying to fit so much work into your day.

Bottled and tinned juices are not as nutritious as freshly made. If you need to make several juices at one time, put the juice in a thermos, filling it to the top and keep it as cool as possible.

This is only a brief outline of the properties that the juices contain. For further reading refer to: *The Uses of Juices*, C.E. Clinkard; *Foods that Heal*, Dr Bernard Jenson; *Green Barley Essence*, Yoshihide Hagiwara.

28-Day Menu Suggestion

This 28-day menu is a suggestion only, to help you see that there can be variety in a vegan-type diet, one that leaves out everything that does not contribute to rebalancing your body through your diet.

You can change the menu around any way you please. There is no definite order to eat it in. If you would rather replace a meal with several juices that is okay. At times it may be better to do that. Trust how you feel.

You may prefer to have your main meal at lunch time. That often fits in better with your lifestle. Eating less in the evening is better for your digestion too.

The recipe quantities are on an average for 2–3 people. If allowing for a big eater use for 2.

There are lists of foods set out here that you need to buy. They will probably last through the 28 days. It seems a lot but you will continue to use them as you change to this pattern of eating. If there does not seem to be enough to eat make bigger quantities; keep meals simple.

If you can drink more juices than are suggested in the menu it will be beneficial. The quantities of vegetables for your juices are included in the weekly greengrocer's list. The actual ingredients in each juice are listed but you can vary them as you please. Juice quantities are for one person only.

Each day's menu is accompanied by recipe suggestions. More recipes for breads, soups, vegetable dishes, sauces, pasta dishes, desserts and cakes begin on page 101.

Helpful hints for the 28-day menu

Try to plan your meal and juice preparation times so you are not tempted to skip the important aspect of nurturing yourself.

If you need to prepare a juice ahead, put it in a thermos flask. Fill to the top and keep as cool as possible.

At the beginning of each week make up half a litre of French salad dressing. Make up a yoghurt/oil mix as well. You can make a savoury mix with the yoghurt and oil. Just leave out the honey and mix in any herbs or savoury flavour that you like.

Have a quantity of simple hommos on hand as well. You can put extra garlic in the hommos and spread it on bread or rolls and heat the same way you would ordinary garlic bread.

Buy some yeast flakes (Red Star is good) and sprinkle them on any food that needs an extra flavour or nutritional lift. These flakes are not the kind that contribute to candida.

When you bring home your green leafy vegetables and parsley, wash and wrap them in white kitchen paper, then put in a plastic bag (the only time we recommend anything to do with plastic) and put in the crisper of your fridge. We have already pointed out that hydroponic lettuces are best left in the shop and that green leafy types of lettuce have many more nutrients than the white iceberg lettuce.

A teaspoon of barley miso in a cup of hot water helps to settle a lot of digestive problems. Miso is very alkalising although it is salty.

A teaspoon of slippery elm powder mixed into a glass of pear juice and drunk first thing in the morning then followed straight away with a hot drink of some kind helps a lot with constipation problems. This can be done several times a day but works best on a fairly empty stomach.

Buy a good chopping knife, one that has at least a 1½ cm 'heel' on it, so that you have room for your fingers to get a good grip.

Remember to soak your porridge and any legumes you will need for the next day.

Don't keep cooked rice or grains any more than 24 hours. They harbour very bad bacteria. A cut onion or raw broken egg has similar problems. Reheated potatoes are not good for you.

If you don't use all of an avocado, dunk the part left in cold tap water and wrap loosely in kitchen paper. They don't seem to brown as quickly with this treatment.

Check that the tofu you buy is not made using magnesium chloride.

If you want to put on weight, have lots of barley soups, oatmeal and carob dishes.

Try growing your own sprouts, as sprouted seeds are an excellent source of many vital nutrients. It's a good idea to do this when fresh green leafy vegetables are not readily available.

Alfalfa is really good for clearing out the residue after eating too much animal protein.

Investigate the use of herbs in healing and also the uses of herbal teas.

Ordinary Ceylon tea, although classed as an antioxidant is also a little constipating, so mix around your teas.

Snip up a few sheets of nori seaweed and keep in a jar ready to sprinkle on your food. The nutrients and benefits of seaweed are excellent.

There is a lot of controversy surrounding soy products, if you have any worries or queries check with your doctor about your particular situation. Soy products are used here at the Centre as an alternative to animal and dairy nutrients, but we do not necessarily recommend everyone should eat them; trust how you feel about soy. Moderation in all foods is a good way to go.

Salads have not been included in the evening meal menu for no reason other than a time factor. If you wish to have a salad instead of any meal or added to the evening meal that is your choice.

A hand held 'food wand', the Bamix type, can be a very useful addition to your kitchen, it can be put into many bowls, jars and saucepan to purée or cream and is very easily washed.

To minimise unwanted toxins try to always start with cold tap water for your cooking and heated drinks.

One Cup of Dry Weight In ...

Almonds	equals 200 grams
Apricots	equals 200 grams
Barley	equals 150 grams
Beans	equals 200 grams
Brown Rice	equals 200 grams
Buckwheat	equals 250 grams
Carob Buds	equals 150 grams
Carob Powder	equals 100 grams
Chick Peas	equals 150 grams
Coconut	equals 100 grams
Couscous	equals 150 grams
Currants	equals 125 grams
Dates	equals 150 grams
Flour Rice	equals 150 grams
Flour Soy	equals 100 grams
Flour W/Meal	equals 150 grams
Great Nth Beans	equals 200 grams
Lentils	equals 250 grams
Lima Beans	equals 150 grams
Millet	equals 250 grams
Oat Bran	equals 100 grams
Polenta	equals 200 grams
Raisins	equals 150 grams
Semolina	equals 200 grams
Soy Comp.	equals 100 grams
Split Peas	equals 150 grams
Sultanas	equals 150 grams
Unproc. Bran	equals 100 grams
Wild Rice	equals 200 grams

Groceries or Dry goods—28 Days

These products are not repeated in weekly shopping lists, they are quantities to last 28 days. Saves buying small amounts each week, cheaper and they keep.

Most herbs and spices can be bought in large quantities but they do lose flavour if kept for any length of time. This amount would last several months.

Agar Agar — 30 g
Almonds — 500 g
Apple Cider Vinegar — ½ lt
Apple Juice — 1 litre
Apricots (Dry) — 250 g
Barley Green Powder — 1 jar
Barley Miso — 1 pkt
Barley Rolled — 500 g
Basil — 25 g
Bay Leaves — 25 g
Bernard Jensens Broth powder — 1 jar
Bran Oat — 200 g
Bran Rice — 200 g
Brown Rice — 1 kg
Buckwheat Kernels — 500 g
Burghul Wheat — 1 pkt
Cannelloni Tubes — 1 pkt
Caraway Seeds — 25 g
Carob Buds — 500 g
Carob Powder — 250 g
Cayenne — 25 g

Chick Peas — 1 kg
Cinnamon — 1 pkt
Coconut — 250 g
Cold Extracted Flax Oil — 500 ml tin
Coriander — 25 g
Corn Flour — 1 pkt
Corn Noodles (instant lasagne) — 1 pkt
Couscous — 1 pkt
Cumin — 25 g
Currants — 500 g
Curry Powder — 1 pkt
Dandelion Coffee Grounds — 100 g
Dates — 350 g
Dill Seeds — 25 g
Eggs — 6
Garum Marsala — 1 pkt
Green Tea — 1 pkt
Haricot Beans — 1 pkt
Horseradish cream — sml jar
Herb Teas your Choice
Herbamare — 1 pkt
Honey — 1 kg
Hulled Millet — 500 g
Jam Unsugared — 6 jars
Kelp Powder — 1 pkt
Kombu — 1 pkt
Lentils — 500 g
Maple Syrup (Pure) — 1 bottle
Marjoram — 25 g
Mayonnaise Soy — 1 kg approx
Mixed Herbs — 25 g
Mixed Spice — 1 pkt
Mustard English — 1 jar
Mustard French — 1 jar
Mustard Seeds — 25 g
Oats Rolled — 1 kg

Olives (Black) — 1 jar
Oregano — 25 g
Parmesan Cheese — sml block
Pasta of choice — 1 pkt
Polenta — 250 g
Poppy Seeds — 25 g
Prunes — 500 g
Raisins — 250 g
Rice Crackers — 2 pkts
Rice Flour — 500 g
Rice Pasta — 2 pkts
Rice Rolled — 200 g
Rice Syrup — 500 g approx
Sage — 25 g
Salt Skip (Baking Powder) — 1 pkt
Slippery Elm Powder — 125 g
Soy Compound — 1 kg
Soy Flour — 250 g
Spaghetti Organic — 1 pkt
Split Peas — 500 g
Sultanas — 500 g
Sun Dried Tomatoes — 1 jar
Sushi Nori — 2 pkts
Sweet Paprika — 25 g
Tamari — 1 sml bottle
Thyme — 25 g
Tomato Puree — 2 jars
Tomato Paste — (375 g approx) small
Triticale Rolled — 500 g
Unpearled Barley — 500 g
Vanilla (Pure) — 1 small bottle
Whole Linseeds — 150 g
Wholemeal Flour — 1 kg
Wild Rice — 1 pkt
Yellow split Peas — 1 pkt

Supermarket/health Food Store and Greengrocer's Shopping List

Perishables for week one

Bread — 1 loaf
Filo Pastry — 1 pkt
Focaccia — 1 large
Fruit Juice — 1 litre
Pita Bread — 4
Rolls — 8
Soy Milk—(or oat milk) — 2 litres
Soy Yoghurt — 250 g
Spaghetti — ½ pkt
Tofu—block — 600 g approx
Alfalfa — 1 carton
Avocado — 3
Beans — 150 g
Beetroot — 3
Broccoli — 1 head
Cabbage — 1
Cantelope (Rockmelon) — 1
Carrots — 10 kg
Cauliflower — 1
Celery—bunch — 1½
Cucumber — 1
Fruit Pieces — 14–16
Garlic—knob — ¼
Ginger—knob — 1
Green Capsicum — 5
Leeks — 2

Lemons — 8
Lettuce — 4–5
Mung Bean Sprouts — 100 g
Mushrooms — 200 g
Onions — 7
Parsley—bunch — 1
Potatoes — 4
Pumpkin — 3 kg
Radish—bunch — 1
Red Cabbage — ¼
Red Capsicum — 2
Red Onion — 1
Spinach—bunch — 1
Spring Onions—bunch — 1
Sweet Potato — 500 g
Tomatoes — 9
Zucchini — 2

Useful Recipes to Make up each week for 28-day menu

Flax oil dressing

5 tbs flax seed oil (cold extracted)
1 small clove garlic crushed
½ tsp mustard
3 tbs apple cider vinegar
½ tsp honey
Combine all ingredients (a Bamix works well). Store in refrigerator.

Hoummos dip or spread

½ cup dry chick-peas (garbanzos)
¼ cup water
2 dsp lemon juice
1 tsp flax seed oil
1 clove crushed garlic
1 dsp tamari

Preparation: 10 min
Cook: 40–50 min

Cover and soak chickpeas overnight in water. Pour off soak water and cover with fresh water. Cook until tender and drain. Blend chickpeas, adding the ¼ cup water and other ingredients gradually. Blend well.

Oil and Soy Yoghurt mix

1 cup soy yoghurt
½ cup cold pressed flax seed oil
1 tsp honey

Put all ingredients in a food processor and process or put in a jar and emulsify with a bamix type mixer for 5 minutes.

The above can be prepared in advance for each week to minimise preparation time each day.

Juices
A guide to quantities for 1 glass of juice.
250 g carrot
or

200 g carrot
2 sticks celery
or
175 g carrot
2 sticks celery
½ beetroot
or
Green leaf:
4–5 lettuce leaves
2 cabbage leaves
2 sticks celery
½ green capsicum
2–4 spinach leaves or beetroot
¼ green apple

. . . .

DAY ONE

ON RISING: Lemon Juice (⅓ cup) and
⅔ cup warm water or 1 cup Dandelion
coffee

BREAKFAST: Porridge with soaked
currants, soy milk or oat milk

10.00 A.M.: Carrot juice

11.00 A.M.: Green juice, either fresh
or powdered green, or a combination of
both

12.00 NOON Carrot, celery and beetroot juice

LUNCH: Salad roll with mayonnaise,

avocado and a sprinkle of nori seaweed

2.30 P.M.: Carrot and celery juice

4.00 P.M.: Fresh or bottled fruit juice
or two pieces of fruit

5.30 P.M.: Green tea (optional) or
another juice

DINNER: Steamed vegetables; cauliflower, broccoli, mushrooms, onions
and garlic with sauce made from a base
of tofu; bread roll with hommos if
liked

Dandelion 'coffee'

Dandelion root 'coffee' is best prepared
by placing ½ cup dandelion coffee
grounds into a stainless steel pot and
adding 1 litre of water. Bring to the boil
and simmer gently for about 2 minutes.
Strain and serve. The grounds can be
reused several times. Add more water
each time it is reheated. Cook a little
longer each time. Keep in a covered
container in the refrigerator between
times.

Porridge

½ cup rolled oats
¼ cup rolled barley
¼ cup rolled triticale
1 dsp linseeds

Soak ingredients, except linseeds, overnight in cold water (enough to cover them 3 cm over). In the morning cook over a gentle heat. Stir constantly, adding more water to enable porridge to fall off the spoon easily. While porridge is cooking, crush the linseeds and add to porridge. Stir well and serve. Adding 2 tbs currants which have been soaked overnight in cold water.

Sauce for steamed vegetables

2 cups water
1 tbs barley miso
1 tsp crushed garlic
1 tsp grated ginger
1 dsp cornflour
$\frac{1}{2}$ block pureed tofu

Boil water, seasonings and cornflour for two minutes. Add tofu (cream tofu in a food processor or with a bamix). Adjust seasoning if necessary and pour over vegetables.

. . . .

DAY TWO

ON RISING: Lemon juice ($\frac{1}{3}$ cup) and $\frac{2}{3}$ cup warm water or 1 cup dandelion coffee

BREAKFAST: Bowl of fruit; banana, apple, pear with soaked sultanas

10.00 A.M.: Carrot juice

11.00 A.M.: Fresh green juice with 1 tsp barley green powder

12.00 NOON: Carrot, celery and beetroot juice

LUNCH: Miso soup with tofu, mung beans and nori; add extra greens to basic soup; bread roll

2.30 P.M.: Carrot and celery juice

4.00 P.M.: Slice of John's cake and herb tea or a piece of fruit

5.30 P.M.: Green tea or 1 glass of carrot juice

DINNER: Legume burgers with mustard cream; sweet potato baked in the oven; green beans

Miso soup base

5 × 5 cm square washed kombu (seaweed)
$1\frac{1}{2}$ cup carrots sliced into $\frac{1}{2}$ moons
1 litre cold water
$\frac{1}{2}$ cup diced cabbage
$\frac{1}{2}$ small onion
1 dsp grated green ginger
1 tbs barley miso
1 spring onion, chopped
$\frac{1}{4}$ cup chopped celery

Preparation: 20 min
Cook: 30 min

Simmer kombu, onion, carrots, cabbage, and celery in 1 litre water for 30 minutes. Take out kombu and chop finely. Return to pot with ginger and miso. Mix but don't boil; serve with spring onions on top. This soup can be varied by adding other vegetables and or noodles, e.g., diced marinated tofu, mung beans, broccoli, pumpkin.

Legume burgers (serves 2–3)

1½ litres water
1 medium onion, chopped
½ cup brown or green lentils
½ cup yellow split peas
½ cup bread crumbs
1 tsp mustard cream
1 tsp horseradish cream
1 tsp dried thyme or 2 tsp chopped fresh thyme

Preparation: 25 min
Cook: 30 min

Put water in a medium size saucepan and heat to boiling. Add lentils, split peas and onion. Simmer gently until soft (about 30 minutes). While lentils are cooking, crumb a slice of wholemeal bread in a food processor or place torn up slice in a jar and break up with Bamix-type mixer. Heat oven to 250°. When the lentils and peas are cooked, drain them,

place in a bowl and mash with a potato masher. Add the rest of the ingredients and shape mixture into patties. Place on a greased tray and put in hot oven. Turn once, about 15 minutes after putting in the oven. Cook a further 15 minutes. (This mixture makes five average size patties.) If you don't use them all they make a nice sandwich filling with some salad for lunch the next day.

Mustard cream sauce

2 tsp mustard seeds
½ cup soy mayonnaise
1 tsp hot English mustard
2 chopped spring onions

Chop spring onions finely. Place the mustard seeds in a heavy based saucepan, put on the heat and shake gently. The seeds will pop as the pan base gets hot. Take off the heat and mix in the other ingredients. Serve over the burgers.

John's cake

⅓ cup brown rice flour
⅓ cup corn flour
⅓ cup soy flour
½ cup coconut
2 tsp salt skip
¾–1 cup soy milk
⅓ cup chopped dried apricots *or* dates
½ cup sultanas
½ cup raisins

Preparation: 25 min
Cook: 30 min

Sift dry ingredients twice, add all other ingredients and place in slab cake tin. Cook in moderate oven for approximately 30 minutes.

. . . .

DAY THREE

ON RISING: Lemon juice (⅓ cup) and ⅔ cup warm water or 1 cup dandelion coffee

BREAKFAST: Porridge with yoghurt and oil mix

10.00 A.M.: Carrot juice

11.00 A.M.: Fresh green juice with 1 tsp of powdered barley green, or any similar green powder

12.00 NOON: Carrot, celery and beetroot juice

LUNCH: Grilled vegetables in focaccia bread with nori

2.30 P.M.: Carrot and parsley juice

4.00 P.M.: Bowl of grapes or 2 pieces of stone fruit or fruit of choice, or a handful of almonds

5.30 P.M.: Green tea

DINNER: Mushroom soup; spaghetti with golden sauce

Focaccia

1 focaccia bread
1 zucchini
½ onion
2 tomatoes
½ green capsicum
3–4 mushrooms
1 tbs tamari

Slice vegetables thinly and place on a greased tray under the grill or put in a pan on top of the stove with the lid on and allow to steam for a while. Split the focaccia and spread with mayonnaise or your favourite spread, e.g. avocado or hoummos. Place the vegetables on one side sprinkle with tamari and put the other half on top. Reheat whole focaccia in the oven if you wish.

Mushroom soup (serves 1)

1½ cups chopped mushrooms
¼ cup chopped onion
¼ cup soy milk
1 dsp tamari
⅓ tsp herbamare
1 cup water

Preparation: 5 min
Cook: 10 min

Put all ingredients, except soy milk, in a saucepan. Cook gently, stirring occasionally till soft. Puree, and add soy milk. Reheat, then serve with a dollop of yoghurt and sprinkle of parsley.

Spaghetti with golden sauce

200 g spaghetti or pasta of choice
2 cups diced pumpkin
2 cups diced sweet potato
2 cups diced carrots
1 tsp cumin powder
1 tsp herbamare
1 tbs chopped parsley
5 tbs fresh grated parmesan cheese

Place vegetables except parsley in a pan and cover with water. Cover pan. Bring vegetables to the boil and simmer till cooked. Stir occasionally. Add herbamare and cumin. When ready puree roughly, leaving a little chunky. Cook pasta as per instructions and drain. Place in bowls and spoon on sauce. Sprinkle with cheese and parsley.

. . . .

DAY FOUR

ON RISING: Lemon juice (⅓ cup) and ⅔ cup warm water or 1 cup dandelion coffee

BREAKFAST: 2–3 slices rye or wholemeal toast, spread with jam, honey or miso

10.00 A.M.: Carrot juice

11.00 A.M.: Green juice

12.00 NOON: Carrot, celery and beetroot juice

LUNCH: Pita bread filled with coleslaw and grated beetroot, lettuce and sprouts

2.30 P.M.: Carrot juice

4.00 P.M.: Carob balls or fruit juice, or a handful of almonds

5.30 P.M.: Green tea

DINNER: Vegetable strudel with basil yoghurt sauce and brown rice with seaweed

Carob balls (makes 20)

½ cup carob powder
1 cup coconut
1 dsp honey
¼ cup sultanas
¾ cup soy compound
¼ cup chopped carob buds
¼ cup chopped almonds or apricots
½ cup water

Preparation: 20 min

Mix all ingredients together, except water. Add enough water to mix to a stiff dough. Roll into balls and then roll in extra coconut or chopped nuts to give an even coating.

Vegetable strudel with basil yoghurt sauce

2 cups shredded cabbage
1 medium carrot, grated
1 tsp caraway seeds
½ medium zucchini, grated
½ medium leek, chopped
¼ cup chopped chives
1 tbs soy yoghurt mixed with 1 tbs mayonnaise
2 tbs plain flour (use rice flour for gluten-free diet)
2 tsp French mustard
2 sheets filo pastry (folded over to result in 4 layers of pastry) approx a square shape

Preparation: 30 min
Cook: 30 min

Mix cabbage, carrot, caraway seeds, zucchini and leek together, saute gently until soft. Add the yoghurt/mayonnaise, chives, flour and mustard and mix through. Lay the filling along the centre of the pastry sheets lengthwise. Fold in the edges and roll up the strudel. Brush with a little melted butter, sprinkle with caraway seeds and bake, uncovered, in a moderate oven for approximately 35 minutes. This quantity makes 1 small strudel roll—2 serves.

Basil yoghurt sauce

1 tbs mayonnaise
1 tbs soy yoghurt
1 dsp chopped fresh basil

Combine all ingredients together.

. . . .

DAY FIVE

ON RISING: Lemon juice (⅓ cup) in ⅔ cup warm water or 1 cup dandelion coffee

BREAKFAST: Porridge with soaked currants, soy milk or oat milk

10.00 A.M.: Carrot juice

11.00 A.M.: Fresh green juice or cauliflower soup if weather is cold

12.00 NOON: Carrot, celery and beet-root juice

LUNCH: Avocado salsa with mixed lettuce leaves, olives and nori

2.30 P.M.: Carrot juice

4.00 P.M.: Slice of John's cake or 2

pieces of fruit or a glass of fruit juice

5.30 P.M.: Green tea

DINNER: Wholemeal crepes filled with cauliflower in white sauce and steamed broccoli

Avocado salsa

$^1/_2$ medium red onion
2 large avocados
1 small tomato
$^1/_2$ small red capsicum
$^1/_2$ tsp lemon juice
$^1/_4$ tsp each ground cumin and ground coriander
2 tbs flax seed oil
$^1/_4$ tsp sweet paprika
1 tbs fresh coriander leaves (optional)

Preparation: 20 min

Finely chop red onion and tomato. Peel and large dice avocados. Place coriander and cumin powder in a small pan and gently dry roast stirring until warm, this will release the flavours, cool and add to all other ingredients, mix gently and refrigerate until needed.

Cauliflower crepes (makes 4)

Crepe batter
$^3/_4$ cup wholemeal plain flour
1 egg (optional)

$^1/_4$ tsp herbamare or vegetable salt
$^1/_2$ tsp salt skip
$^1/_4$ cup each soy milk and water (Depending on dryness of the flour, enough to mix flour and egg to a thin cream consistency.)

Preparation: 10 min
Cook: 10 min

Cauliflower sauce

1 cup chopped steamed cauliflower per person
2 tbs chopped spring onion
$^1/_2$ cup white sauce as per recipe for each person
$^1/_2$ tsp herbamare
$^1/_2$ tbs chopped parsley

Preparation: 10 min

Preheat a crepe pan or stainless steel frying pan. Lightly grease with unsalted butter. Pour into pan enough batter to form a thin 15 cm circle. Allow to cook till small bubbles rise (30 to 40 seconds). Turn over and finish cooking. Make 3 more. Keep warm. Heat the sauce and add half to cauliflower, onion, salt and parsley. Divide cauliflower into four portions and place on each crepe, roll up, and ladle the other half of the sauce over rolled crepes. Grate parmesan cheese on as they are served (optional).

DAY SIX

ON RISING: Lemon juice (⅓ cup) in ⅔ cup warm water or 1 cup dandelion coffee

BREAKFAST: ½ cantaloupe or 2–3 pieces of fruit of your choice

10.00 A.M.: Carrot juice

11.00 A.M.: Miso broth with rice crackers or a juice

12.00 NOON: Carrot, celery and beet-root juice

LUNCH: Plate of mixed salad vegetables and salad dressing; two slices of rye or wholemeal bread

2.30 P.M.: Carrot juice with a dash of green ginger

4.00 P.M.: Fruit of your choice (2 pieces) or one glass of juice

5.30 P.M.: Green tea

DINNER: Pumpkin soup; baked potato; yoghurt with spring onion; sauerkraut; tomato and leaf salad

Miso broth

1 tsp barley miso
1 cup hot water

Combine ingredients together, stirring well.

Pumpkin soup

1 kg pumpkin
1 onion
1 tsp herbamare
1 tsp cumin
water to cover

Chop pumpkin and onion roughly. Add seasoning and enough water to cover. Cover and simmer till vegetables are soft. Puree with a Bamix. Add a little soy milk (optional).

Sauerkraut

½ cup chopped red cabbage
1 cup chopped green cabbage
½ cup chopped red onion
1 tbs apple cider vinegar
1 tsp honey
1 clove garlic chopped
½ tsp dill seed or tips

Preparation: 20 min
Cook: 15 min

Combine cabbages, garlic, onion and dill seed. Cook gently for a few

LEFT: Lunch — Pita bread filled with salad   (page 67)

CENTRE TOP: Dinner — Brown rice

CENTRE BOTTOM: Dinner — Vegetable strudel (page 68)

TOP: Lunch — Avocado salsa and salad (page 69)

CENTRE FRONT: Dinner — Wholemeal crepes with cauliflower filling and white sauce (page 69)

FROM TOP LEFT: Lunch — Tofu burger in sorj bread with salad (page 125)

FRONT: Dinner — Carrot lentil loaf (page 76)

BOTTOM LEFT: Lunch — Rice and Vegetable Sushi (page 119)

BOTTOM RIGHT: Dinner — Frittata (page 78)

TOP RIGHT: Dinner — Salsa verde (page 78) and rice pasta

minutes in ½ cup water. Add the 1 tbs apple cider vinegar and the honey prior to serving. Can be served hot or cold.

Baked potato

Potato per person
Cook: 1 hr

Scrub the required amount of potatoes. Prick with a fork several times. Place on oven tray or in a casserole dish. Cover. Place in moderate oven and let steam till nearly done. Remove cover and let brown a little.

. . . .

DAY SEVEN

ON RISING: Lemon juice (⅓ cup) in ⅔ cup warm water or 1 cup dandelion coffee

BREAKFAST: Porridge; some soaked almonds and sultanas

10.00 A.M.: Carrot juice

11.00 A.M.: Fresh green juice with 1 tsp powdered barley green

12.00 NOON: Carrot, celery and beet-root juice

LUNCH: Pizza made using pitta bread;

spread with tomato puree; top with grated carrot, onion, tomato and capsicum and a few olives; grate on some tofu, then sprinkle with tamari; pop in oven for 20–30 minutes

2.30 P.M.: Carrot and celery juice

4.00 P.M.: Fruit (2 pieces)

5.30 P.M.: Green tea or a vegetable juice

DINNER: Rice or spaghetti pasta with lentil bolognaise

Spaghetti or rice pasta with lentil sauce (250 g rice pasta serves 2–3 people)

Either green or brown lentils can be used for the sauce of this recipe. Lentils make an excellent introduction for a non-vegetarian to the dried bean and pea family because they are high in protein, very adaptable, easy to digest and, do not overpower other flavours in the recipe.

½ cup uncooked brown or green lentils
1 medium onion, finely chopped
2½ cups diced mushrooms
1¼ cups peeled and chopped tomatoes
2 tbs tomato puree
2 tbs water
2 cloves garlic, crushed
½ tsp dried marjoram

1 small bay leaf
1 tbs tamari or soy sauce

Preparation: 40 min
Cook: 25 min

Place the lentils in a saucepan of water. Bring uncovered, to a boil, skim, cover, and simmer for about 30 minutes or until soft. Drain. Heat the 2 tbs water in a saucepan and soften the onion and garlic for 4–5 minutes. Add mushrooms, cooked lentils, marjoram and bay leaf and cook for 10 minutes.
Stir in the tomatoes and tomato puree. Cover and cook for 20–25 minutes. Remove the bay leaf and mash the lentil mix to a sauce consistency. Season with tamari. Cook the spaghetti in a large saucepan of boiling water for about 8–10 minutes or until just tender. Drain. Pour the sauce over the cooked spaghetti. Sprinkle with chopped parsley.

Perishables for week two

Apple Juice — 1
Fettuccini — ½ pkt
Fruit Loaf — ½
Rolls — 6
Rye Bread — ½ loaf
Sorj Bread (Mountain bread) — 4 slices
Soy Milk—carton — 2
Soy Yoghurt — ½

Tofu Block — 1
Alfalfa
Avocado — 1
Bananas — 2
Beans — ¼ kg
Beetroot — 7
Cabbage — 1
Carrots — 10 kg
Celery—bunch — 1½
Cherry Tomatoes — 1 pkt
Cooking Apples — 4
Corn — 2
Cucumber — 1
Fruit Pieces — 8–10
Garlic—Knob — ½
Green Capsicum — 6
Leeks — 2
Lemons — 8
Lettuce — 4–5
Melons — 2
Mushrooms — 100 g
Onions — 7
Parsley—bunch — ½
Pears — 4
Potatoes — 9
Red Capsicum — 4
Red Onion — 1
Spring Onions—bunch — 1
Sprouts (mung) — 100 g
Spinach — 1 bunch
Snow Peas — 50 g
Swede — 1
Sweet Potato — 200 g
Tomatoes — 12
Turnip — 1
Zucchini — 3

DAY EIGHT

ON RISING: Lemon juice (⅓ cup) and ⅔ cup warm water or 1 cup dandelion coffee

BREAKFAST: Bowl of prunes. Fruit toast with jam or honey

10.00 A.M.: Carrot juice

11.00 A.M.: Fresh green juice or sprout soup if cold

12.00 NOON: Carrot, celery and beet-root juice

LUNCH: Tofu millet salad; lettuce and small spinach leaves

2.00 P.M.: Carrot and celery juice

4.00 P.M.: Smoothie

5.30 P.M.: Green tea or a vegetable juice

DINNER: Ratatouille and corn cakes

Prunes

Cook required amount of prunes in water for 30 minutes.

Banana smoothie

1 banana
2 tbs soy yoghurt
1 tsp honey
1 cup soy milk (organic preferably)
1 tsp slippery elm powder

Preparation: 5 min

Blend together well, sip slowly. Soaked dried fruits may be substituted for bananas.

Tofu millet salad

A spicy fragrant tofu and millet salad, delicious as a main course or lunch. Millet is high in protein and is a non-mucus forming grain.

2 cups cooked millet
1 red pepper, julienne
1 green pepper, julienne
2 spring onions, cut fine on angle
1 tsp fresh grated ginger
300 g cubed firm tofu, marinated in 50:50 tamari and water for approx 1 hour then drain
1 tbs lemon juice
1 small garlic clove
2 tsp tamari

Preparation: 25 min
Cook: 30 min

Mix all ingredients together gently.

73

Ratatouille with corn cakes
(serves 2)

Ratatouille
½ medium onion chopped
½ chopped red capsicum
½ chopped green capsicum
2 medium tomatoes
1 medium zucchini sliced
⅓ cup fresh basil chopped or 1 tsp dried basil
2 tbs water
1 tsp garlic

Preparation: 15 min
Cook: 15 min

Saute garlic and onion in the water. Add zucchini, tomatoes and capsicum. Simmer with lid on until vegies are cooked. Meanwhile make corncakes on a grill or frypan.

Corn cakes

1 cup rice flour
corn from 2 cobs
2 tsp salt skip
1 egg
½ tsp herbamare
1 tsp chopped garlic
1 tbs sliced spring onions
1 tsp mixed herbs
¾ cup soy milk (approx)

Preparation: 10 min
Cook: 10 min

Sift flour and salt skip, add corn, make a well in the centre of the flour and add the milk, egg and seasonings. You may need a little more milk to make a mix that will drop easily on the pan. Put ¼ cup of mix on a heated greased pan, cook till bubbles appear, turn over and cook a little longer, repeat process to use all mix. Serve hot with ratatouille. Sprinkle with chopped basil or a herb of choice.

Sprout Soup

1 onion, chopped
1 stick celery, sliced
4 cups water
1 cup mung beans sprouts
1 carrot cut into thin sticks
4 mushrooms, sliced
2 flat tbs barley miso

In a saucepan boil the onion, carrot, celery, and water for 5 minutes. Add mung beans and mushrooms. Boil 2 minutes, take off heat and stir in the miso.

. . . .

DAY NINE

ON RISING: Lemon juice (⅓ cup) and ⅔ cup warm water or 1 cup dandelion coffee

BREAKFAST: Porridge with soy or oat milk and honey

10.00 A.M.: Carrot juice

11.00 A.M.: Fresh green juice and 1 tsp barley green powder

12.00 NOON: Carrot, celery and beet-root juice

LUNCH: Plate of salad with avocado and dressing

2.30 P.M.: Carrot juice

4.00 P.M.: Carob cookies; herb tea or dandelion coffee

5.30 P.M.: Green tea or a vegetable juice

DINNER: Tofu rice burgers with hoummos, green beans and peas; make enough burgers to use in tomorrow's lunch

Tofu rice burgers (makes 6)

½ block tofu
2 tbs chopped parsley
1 dsp mixed herbs
¼ cup chopped spring onions
½ cup grated carrot
Tamari
Garlic
1 cup cooked rice (puree ½ rice after cooking)

Preparation: 25 min

Cook: 20 min

Mash tofu and mix all ingredients together, make into 6 burgers, place on greased tray and brown in fairly hot oven, for about 20 minutes.

Carob cookies

½ cup wholemeal or brown rice flour
½ cup oat bran
½ cup wheat bran or rice bran
½ cup dates
1 cup apple juice
1 cup carob buds (chop if they are large)
1 tbs baking powder (salt skip or other substitute)
1 dsp vanilla

Heat oven to 200°. Pulse chop the dates with the apple juice in a food processor. Add vanilla and the rest of the ingredients. Pulse chop for a few moments. Turn mixture into a bowl and add the carob chips. Mix well and roll dough into 2½ cm balls. Put on a greased tray and flatten a little with a fork. Cook about 15 minutes.

. . . .

DAY TEN

ON RISING: Lemon juice (⅓ cup) and ⅔ cup warm water or 1 cup dandelion coffee

BREAKFAST: Stewed fruit (apple or pears); soy yoghurt and oil mix; toast if needed

10.00 A.M.: Carrot juice

11.00 A.M.: Fresh green juice and barley green powder

12.00 NOON: Carrot, celery and beetroot juice

LUNCH: Sorj bread rolled around a tofu burger with hommos and salad

2.30 P.M.: Carrot and celery juice

4.00 P.M.: Fruit (2 pieces)

5.30 P.M.: Green tea

DINNER: Carrot lentil loaf with onion gravy; mixed steamed vegetables (carrots, parsnips, celery, turnip, onion)

Carrot and lentil loaf

2 cups diced carrots
1/2 cup lentils uncooked
1/2 cup finely chopped onion, or spring onions
1/2 cup chopped almonds
1 cup rolled oats
1/2 tsp sage
2 tbs tamari
2 tbs chopped parsley

1 tsp herbamare (optional)

Preparation: 45 min
Cook: 45 min

Steam carrots. Cook and drain lentils. Mash carrots and lentils, then add to all other ingredients. Pack into a greased loaf pan. Bake in a moderate oven (200°) for approximately 45 minutes. Let the loaf stand for 5 minutes when removed from oven, then turn out on to platter. Slice, decorate, etc., before serving.

This recipe makes one loaf, enough for 6 serves. Left-over slices are nice served cold with salad or in a sandwich.
NOTE: Other vegetables may be substituted for carrots—just make up to the cups required. If vegetables are very soft type (e.g. zucchini) be sure to squeeze out excess liquid after steaming them, otherwise the loaf will not hold together.

Onion gravy

1 medium onion roughly chopped
Jensen's broth
1/2 tsp chopped garlic
2 cups water
1/2 tsp mixed herbs
1 tbs corn flour

Preparation: 5 min
Cook: 10 min

Boil all together, except corn flour, until onion is cooked. Thicken with corn flour blended with a little cold water.

. . . .

DAY ELEVEN

ON RISING: Lemon juice (⅓ cup) and
⅔ cup warm water or 1 cup dandelion
coffee

BREAKFAST: Porridge with soy or oat
milk. Soaked almonds

10.00 A.M.: Carrot juice

11.00 A.M.: Fresh green juice and
barley green

12.00 NOON: Carrot, celery and beetroot juice

LUNCH: Mock salmon sushi; spinach
salad

2.30 P.M.: Carrot and celery juice

4.00 P.M.: Carob cookies

5.30 P.M.: Green tea

DINNER: Frittata with savoury rice and
salsa verde

Mock salmon sushi (makes 2 fat rolls using whole sheet nori)

2 sheets (toasted) sushi nori seaweed
⅓ cup minced celery
1 cup finely grated carrots
¼ cup green onions, chopped
1 cup almonds soaked in water overnight
then ground finely
1 tbs liquid aminos, tamari or bouillon
1 tsp kelp powder
3 tbs lemon juice

Preparation: 30 min

Finely grate the carrots in a food processor. Place chop blade in the processor,
then put the carrots and the remaining
ingredients in and pulse chop. Scrape
down the sides of the bowl, then
continue to pulse chop for a couple of
minutes. Divide mix in 2. Roll mixture
in toasted nori, cut each roll in three.
Refrigerate for one hour.

Spinach salad

2 cups lightly packed spinach leaves
4 black olives sliced
4 cherry tomatoes halved
½ cup sliced cucumber
2 tbs toasted almonds sliced

Preparation: 15 min

Mix well and serve with garlic dressing.

Frittata

¼ block tofu, approx 130 g
¼ cup soy milk
1 dsp mixed herbs
1 tsp oregano
½ tsp herbamare
1 slice of sorj bread
½ cup each sliced potato, carrot, pumpkin and onion
1 tbs chopped parsley
barley miso

Preparation: 25 min
Cook: 45 min
Preheat oven to 180° celsius. Grease a 21 cm pie plate with unsalted butter and line with the sorj bread. Lightly steam potato, carrot, pumpkin and onion. Blend together the tofu, soy milk, mixed herbs, oregano, herbamare and bouillon with a food processor or Bamix. Place vegetables together in a bowl with the sauce. Mix gently and place in pie plate on top of the sorj bread. Cover top with slices of tomato then sprinkle with bread crumbs. Bake for 1 hour or till set.
Serve with brown rice flavoured with tamari and spring onions.

Salsa Verde

1 cup chopped tomatoes
½ cup chopped black olives
½ cup chopped spring onions
1 tbs chopped fresh basil
1 tsp chopped garlic

Mix all together.

. . . .

DAY TWELVE

ON RISING: Lemon juice (⅓ cup) and ⅔ cup warm water or 1 cup dandelion coffee

BREAKFAST: Half canteloupe or ½ grapefruit or 2 pieces of fruit; toast if needed. If having canteloupe have on its own please.

10.00 A.M.: Carrot juice

11.00 A.M.: Guacamole and rice crackers or a juice

12.00 NOON: Carrot, celery and beetroot juice

LUNCH: Mexican rice with green salad vegetables

2.30 P.M.: Carrot and celery juice

4.00 P.M.: Fruit (2 pieces) or 1 glass of fruit juice

5.30 P.M.: Green tea

DINNER: Potato and leek soup; fettuccine with tomato sauce

Guacamole

1 large ripe avocado
1 small tomato chopped
1 dsp lemon juice
shake of herbamare
½ tsp crushed garlic
1 tbs chopped parsley or chives
pinch cayenne (optional)
pinch paprika

Preparation: 10 min

Peel and mash avocado. Add other ingredients and blend to a smooth consistency.

Mexican rice (serves 2)

¾ cup wild rice
1 small onion chopped
2 tbs tomato puree
1 small carrot, sliced
½ cup sliced snow peas
1 small tomato, chopped
1 clove garlic chopped
2 cups water or stock
1 tbs chopped red capsicum
1 tbs chopped fresh coriander

Preparation: 20 min
Cook: 45 min

Cook wild rice in stock or water. Saute onion in small amount of water, add other ingredients except snow peas, tomato puree and coriander. Cook, covered until carrot is tender, about 10 minutes. Drain. Mix rice and vegies together, add snow peas and coriander. Pour tomato puree over rice mix and serve.

Potato and leek soup

2 cups sliced leeks
2 cups diced potato
½ clove crushed garlic
1 medium onion
½ litre water
¼ tsp herbamare

Preparation: 5 min
Cook: 10 min

Bring water to boil, add potato and leeks, garlic and herbamare. Cover and simmer until cooked. Blend and thin with water or soy milk if necessary.

Fettuccine noodles

½ pkt fettuccine noodles
2 quantities tomato sauce
½ cup chopped parsley
½ cup fresh grated parmesan cheese

Preparation: 15 min
Cook: 30 min

Make tomato sauce. Grate cheese and chop parsley. Boil noodles in plenty of water till tender. Strain and serve topped with sauce, parsley and cheese.

Tomato sauce

1 cup chopped tomatoes
1 cup stock or water
1 dsp corn flour mixed with cold water
2 tbs tomato puree
1 cup chopped onions
1 clove garlic
2 tbs chopped basil
1 tsp herbamare

Cook all together except corn flour for 10 minutes. Puree and return to pot. Add corn flour and boil one minute.

. . . .

DAY THIRTEEN

ON RISING: Lemon juice (⅓ cup) and ⅔ cup warm water or 1 cup dandelion coffee

BREAKFAST: Porridge with yoghurt and oil mix

10.00 A.M.: Carrot juice

11.00 A.M.: Fresh green juice and 1 tsp barley green powder

12.00 NOON: Carrot, celery and beetroot juice

LUNCH: Barley vegetable soup with wholemeal roll or toast

2.30 P.M.: Carrot and celery juice

4.00 P.M.: Special fruit salad

5.30 P.M.: Carrot juice

DINNER: Polenta with mushroom sauce; beetroot salad

Barley vegetable soup (serves 2)

2 tbs unpearled barley
½ cup onions
1 small potato
½ cup carrots
¼ cup parsnip
¼ cup turnip
¼ cup swede
½ stick celery
750 ml water
⅓ tsp each basil, marjoram, oregano
½ tsp garlic
1 dsp Jensens vegetable seasoning
1 tbs chopped parsley
1 bay leaf

Preparation: 20 min
Cook: 1½ hrs

Chop vegetables. Cook barley, onions, potatoes, and carrots with bay leaf in water for about 1 hour. Then add remaining ingredients. Cook further ½ hour for best results. Add more water as needed. Add bouillon, top with parsley and serve with crusty bread or toast.

Polenta with mushroom sauce

½ cup cooked brown rice
1 cup vegetable stock or water
½ cup soy or oat milk
½ cup polenta
¼ cup toasted, chopped almonds
½ tsp herbamare
2 tsp chopped fresh basil or 1 tsp dried basil

Preparation: 40 min
Cook: 45 min

Bring stock and milk to boil in a pan, stir in polenta and simmer about 10 minutes stirring constantly. Add rice, almonds, basil and herbamare. Mix well. Spread mixture evenly on baking tray. Mark into triangles. Cook in a moderate oven 10–15 minutes. Serves 2–3.

Mushroom sauce

100 g sliced mushrooms
6 chopped spring onions
½ cup uncooked chick peas
1 cup stock or water
½ cup mayonnaise
2 tsp crushed garlic
2 tsp corn flour blended in a little water
2 tsp tamari
¼ cup soy yoghurt

Preparation: 15 min
Cook: 45 min

Soak chick peas overnight. Drain and cook in fresh water for approximately 45 minutes or till tender. Saute mushrooms, onions and garlic in a little water. Add other ingredients. Bring to boil and simmer 2–3 minutes. Serve over polenta triangles, topped with chopped parsley or spring onions.

Special fruit salad (serves 2–3)

2 pears
2 figs, fresh or 4 dried (optional)
8 dates
¼ cup coconut
½ cup chopped almonds

Chop all fruit and add coconut and almonds. Serve with a dollop of yoghurt.

Warm beetroot salad

2 large beetroot

Scrub and cook beetroot, then slip off skin, dice beetroot. (If preferred, peel and dice beetroot before cooking).

Dressing

1 tbs chopped red onion
1 medium chopped cucumber
2 tbs cider vinegar
2 tsp dill seed
2 tsp honey
2 chopped spring onions

Mix dressing ingredients and pour over hot beetroot just prior to serving.

Perishables for week three

Bread—loaf — ¼
Currants — 500 g
Dried Apricots — 300 g
Focaccia — 2
Fruit Bread Loaf — ½
Pita Bread — 2
Prunes — 200 g
Rolled Oats — 500 g
Rolls — 6
Soy Milk — 3 litres
Soy Yoghurt — 300–400 ml
Sultanas — 500 g
Tofu—block — 400 g approx.
Alfalfa—punnet — 1
Avocado — 1
Beans — ¼ kg
Beetroot — 5
Broccoli — 1 head
Brussel Sprouts — ½ kg
Cabbage — 1
Carrots — 10 kg
Cauliflower — 1
Celery—bunch — 1½
Cucumber — 2
Fruit Pieces — 8–10
Garlic—Knob — ½
Grape Fruit — 2
Green Capsicum — 2
Lemons — 12
Lettuce — 5
Mint—bunch — 1
Mung Bean Sprouts — 100 g
Mushrooms — 100 g

Onions — 6
Parsley—bunch — 1
Parsnip — 1
Potatoes — 4
Pumpkin — 2 kg
Radish—bunch — 1
Red Capsicum — 2
Snow Peas — ½ kg
Spinach—bunch — 2
Spring Onions—bunch — 1
Sprouts—punnet — 1
Sweet Potato — 2
Tomatoes — 12
Zucchini — 5

. . . .

DAY FOURTEEN

ON RISING: Lemon juice (⅓ cup) and ⅔ cup warm water or 1 cup dandelion coffee

BREAKFAST: Rye or wholemeal bread toasted with jam, honey or miso spread

10.00 A.M.: Carrot juice

11.00 A.M.: Fresh green juice with barley green

12.00 NOON: Carrot, celery and beetroot juice

LUNCH: Potato salad; tomato, lettuce and alfalfa

2.30 P.M.: Carrot, celery and beetroot juice

4.00 P.M.: Melons

5.30 P.M.: Green tea or a juice

DINNER: Ratatouille parcels with tomato or yoghurt/dill sauce; mashed sweet potato

Potato salad

¼ cup diced celery
2 dsp soy yoghurt
1 dsp finely chopped red onion
2 cups cubed boiled, cooled, new potatoes
1 dsp French dressing
1 dsp freshly chopped dill or 1 tsp dill seed
¼ tsp French mustard
Pinch dill tips to serve on top

Preparation: 10 min
Cook: 20 min

Mix together the dill, yoghurt, mustard and French dressing. Toss with the potatoes, celery and onion. Serve chilled.

Ratatouille parcels (serves 2)

4 large cabbage, lettuce or silverbeet leaves
1 cup diced zucchini

1 cup diced onions cooked
1 cup diced carrots
1 cup diced tomato
1 tsp herbamare or vegetable salt
1 tsp crushed garlic

Preparation: 30 min
Cook: 1 hr

Cut hard centre stalk from cabbage or silverbeet leaves and steam them for 5 minutes approximately, just until they are soft and pliable. Rinse under cold water. Mix diced vegetables and add seasonings. Divide vegetables in four portions. Place on cabbage leaves and roll up in a parcel, making sure to tuck in the ends of each roll as you go. Place together in a greased casserole dish and cover, cook in a moderate oven for about ¾ hour. Serve with tomato or yoghurt and dill sauce. Accompany with a cooked grain e.g. barley or rice and mashed sweet potato.

. . . .

DAY FIFTEEN

ON RISING: Lemon juice (⅓ cup) and ⅔ cup warm water or 1 cup dandelion coffee

BREAKFAST: Porridge with soy or oat milk

10.00 A.M.: Carrot juice

11.00 A.M.: Broth made with mineral bouillon; rice crackers

12.00 NOON: Carrot, celery and beetroot juice

LUNCH: Pita bread filled with left over potato salad, lettuce, tomato and celery; extra mayonnaise, red and green capsicum.

2.30 P.M.: Carrot and celery juice

4.00 P.M.: Fruit of choice (2 pieces)

5.30 P.M.: Green tea

DINNER: Steamed vegetables with curry and yoghurt sauce; couscous

Broth
_____

1 tsp mineral bouillon
1 cup hot water

Mix ingredients together stirring well.

Steamed vegetables with curry and yoghurt sauce (serves 1–2)
_____

100 g snow peas
1 cup sliced carrots
½ cup sliced onion
1 dsp curry powder
1 cup chopped cauliflower florets

1 cup sliced cucumber
150 ml soy yoghurt
pinch herbamare

Preparation: 15 min
Cook: 15 min

Steam vegetables. Saute onion in a little water till transparent. Add curry powder and herbamare and cook a little longer; add soy yoghurt and heat gently. Pour the warm sauce over the hot steamed vegetables and serve with 1 cup cooked brown rice or couscous.

Minted couscous (serves 2)
_____

½ cup couscous soaked in 1 cup hot water
2 spring onions chopped
1½ tbs chopped fresh parsley
1½ tbs chopped fresh mint
1 tbs tamari
1 tbs flax seed oil
1 tbs lemon juice
2 tomatoes sliced
black olives

Preparation: 45 min

Soak the couscous for 30 minutes. Drain and dry well on kitchen paper. Add the spring onions, parsley, mint, tamari, flax seed oil, lemon juice and mix well. Reheat in oven if liked warm. Garnish with tomato slices and black olives.

DAY SIXTEEN

ON RISING: Lemon juice (⅓ cup) and ⅔ cup warm water or 1 cup dandelion coffee

BREAKFAST: Dried fruit soaked and cooked with almonds and cinnamon

10.00 A.M.: Carrot juice

11.00 A.M.: Fresh green juice or miso broth

12.00 NOON: Carrot, celery and beetroot juice

LUNCH: Tabouleh with hommos in pita or sorj bread

2.30 P.M.: Carrot and celery juice

4.00 P.M.: Fruit cake or piece of fruit

5.30 P.M.: Green tea

DINNER: Falafel with hommos; broccoli and cauliflower

Tabouleh salad (serves 2)

1 cup burghal wheat or couscous
1 cup finely chopped onion
1 cup finely chopped parsley
½ cup finely chopped fresh mint
2 tomatoes finely chopped
½ cucumber finely chopped
4 tbs flax oil
4 tbs lemon juice

Preparation: 20 min

Soak burghal or couscous for 2 hours in warm water. Tip into a sieve or colander lined with a clean cloth. Twist the cloth around and squeeze to extract all the moisture. Turn into a large bowl and knead in the onion with your hand for a couple of minutes. Add other ingredients; mix gently and thoroughly into the mixture and chill for one hour. Pile on to a bed of lettuce. Garnish with olives or nasturtium leaves and flowers if you have some. If at the chilling stage you press the mixture down well into an oiled bowl or simple jelly mould, it will keep its shape when inverted on to a serving plate and given a firm tap.

Falafel

1 cup chick peas (2 when soaked)
¼ cup finely chopped chives or spring onions
1 crushed garlic clove
¼ cup finely chopped parsley
1 small carrot finely grated
¼ cup cooked rice
2 tbs water
¼ tsp paprika
1 tbs cider vinegar
1 tsp cumin

1 tsp coriander
1 tbs tamari
1 tsp garam marsala

Preparation: 25 min
Cook: 25 min

Soak peas overnight, drain and cover with fresh water and cook until tender. Put through food processor until fine texture is obtained. Add other ingredients and roll into balls flattened slightly, coating with bran or bread crumbs or wholemeal flour. Bake on lightly greased tray at 180° for 20 minutes. Serve with hommos.

Fruit cake

1½ cups raisins
1½ cups dried apricots (chop roughly)
1½ cups almonds
1½ cups currants
1½ cups sultanas
3 eggs
1 cup dates
¼ cup water
750 g flour (all brown rice or all wholemeal or 50:50)
2 lemons
1 dsp cinnamon
200ml cold water
1 dsp mixed spice
1/4 cup rice syrup

Preheat oven to 180°. Put all fruit except dates together with 500ml of cold water and heat in a saucepan. Heat until steaming. Allow to cool. Roughly chop 1 cup dates and add to ¼ cup of water and bring to boil, then mash with a fork (or better still, a Bamix type mixer). Meanwhile, grate the peel of 2 lemons, then squeeze out the juice. Add to flour 1 dessertspoon cinnamon and 1 dessertspoon mixed spice. Add the lemon rind and juice, date mix and the spices and 3 eggs to the fruit mix, stir well, add ¼ cup of rice syrup and the flour mix. Line a 25 cm cake tin with 4 layers of greased greaseproof paper and fill with the mix. Smooth the top and cook for approximately 1½–2 hours. Allow to cool in the tin, then take out and peel off the paper. Keep in an airtight tin as there is no fat to keep cake moist. This mix can also be used as a Christmas pudding. As there is no sugar or alcohol to preserve it, refrigerate pudding after cooling. If you wish, you can replace some of the water with your choice of alcohol.

. . . .

DAY SEVENTEEN

ON RISING: Lemon juice (⅓ cup) and ⅔ cup warm water or 1 cup dandelion coffee

BREAKFAST: Rolled rice porridge with soy or oat milk; sultanas

CENTRE TOP: Lunch — Barley vegetable soup and roll (page 80)

CENTRE BOTTOM: Dinner — Polenta with mushroom sauce (page 81)
Warm beetroot salad (page 81)

BOTTOM LEFT: Lunch – Corn chowder and salad (page 109)

BOTTOM RIGHT: Dinner – Sweet and sour tofu and vegetables (page 94)

FROM TOP: Brown rice, wholemeal toast, Parsnip soup (page 99)

FRONT: Spanikopita with mushroom sauce (page 99)

TOP: Lunch — Half avocado and salad

BOTTOM LEFT: Dinner — Sweet potato roulade and potato chips (page 95)

10.00 A.M.: Carrot juice

11.00 A.M.: Fresh green juice and 1 tsp barley green powder

12.00 NOON: Carrot, celery and beet-root juice

LUNCH: Salad with mixed sprouts and avocado

2.30 P.M.: Carrot and celery juice

4.00 P.M.: Fruit of choice (2 pieces)

5.30 P.M.: Green tea

DINNER: Tofu quiche with breadcrumb pastry; green beans and millet

Rolled rice porridge

1 cup rolled rice
Soak overnight in enough water to cover. When required place on stove in a sauce-pan and heat gently, stirring all the time. Simmer for 2 or 3 minutes adding more water if necessary.

Tofu quiche (serves 3–4)

2 tbs lemon juice
$\frac{1}{4}$ cup water or broth
$\frac{1}{2}$ cup each capsicum and onion chopped
$\frac{3}{4}$ cup tomato puree
3 cups zucchini, sliced

Custard

2 garlic cloves
$1\frac{1}{4}$ cups soy milk
$\frac{1}{4}$ cup water or 1 egg
1 tsp herbamare
1 cup tofu, mashed
1 tsp each garlic and cumin
2 tbs arrowroot powder or cornflour

Crust for quiche

3 cups bread crumbs
1 cup hommos
Enough water to mix to a soft dough

Mix together to make the crust
Press over base and sides of pie plate or shallow casserole.

Preparation: 45 min
Cook: 45 min

Preheat oven to 200°. Put lemon juice and water in a large skillet. Heat and add vegies. Cover, saute for 8 minutes on medium. Put tofu custard ingredients together in a blender and blend until smooth and creamy. Stir in tomato puree by hand. To assemble, spread vegies over crust, then poor tofu custard on top. Bake 200° for 45 minutes (or until firm).

DAY EIGHTEEN

ON RISING: Lemon juice (⅓ cup) and ⅔ cup warm water or 1 cup dandelion coffee

BREAKFAST: Porridge with soy or oat milk; currants

10.00 A.M.: Carrot juice

11.00 A.M.: Fresh green juice

12.00 NOON: Carrot, celery and beet-root juice

LUNCH: Miso soup with tofu, mung beans and nori; some extra vegetables i.e. pumpkin and broccoli; bread or roll

2.30 P.M.: Carrot juice with a little green ginger

4.00 P.M.: Fruit cake (1 slice) or piece of fruit

5.30 P.M.: Green tea

DINNER: Minestrone soup; vegetable lasagne; garlic rolls

Minestrone soup (serves 2–4)

1 small onion
½ cup diced carrot
¼ cup chopped celery
½ cup sliced zucchini
½ cup chopped fresh tomatoes
½ cup sliced cabbage
4 cups water
½ tsp honey
1 tsp minced garlic
1 tbs freshly chopped parsley
1 tbs chopped green capsicum
½ tsp dried basil
¼ cup tomato paste
½ tsp dried thyme
½ tsp dried oregano
¼ cup cooked haricot (or beans of choice)

Preparation: 20 min
Cook: 40 min

Braise onions, garlic, carrots and herbs in some of the water until onions are soft. Add the celery, capsicum, cabbage and the rest of the water, simmer for five minutes. Add the tomatoes, paste and beans. Bring to the boil. Lower the heat and continue to cook for 20 minutes, adding more water if needed. Add zucchini and parsley and simmer for another 5 minutes. This makes enough for two large bowls of soup and eaten with a crusty roll makes a satisfying meal.

Lasagne (serves 2)

6–8 sheets of instant corn lasagne noodles

1 cup chopped spinach
1 tomato sliced
2 cups grated pumpkin
½ medium onion

Sauce
4 medium tomatoes
1 small onion
½ cup tomato puree
1 tsp each of basil, oregano, sage
and garlic
½ cup water

Preparation: 30 min
Cook: 45 min

Chop tomatoes and onion. Put in a sauce-pan with the rest of ingredients, and simmer for 15 minutes. When cooked, mash well or puree with a Bamix. Reserve ⅓ of the sauce to serve over the lasagne. Preheat oven 200°. While the sauce is cooking wash and blanch spinach, then drain. Chop, peel and grate pumpkin. Peel and slice onion thinly. Grease an oblong pyrex dish 20 × 10 cm with unsalted butter. Spoon a thin layer of tomato sauce into the base of the casse-role dish, cover with a sheet of lasagne, break to fit dish, if necessary. On this, put a layer of spinach then a few slices of onion, follow with a layer of lasagne, more sauce and layer of pumpkin with a shake of herbamare. Layer of lasagne, sauce, spinach, onion, lasagne, then sauce. Finish off with a layer of pumpkin and herbamare. Cover with greased greaseproof paper and put in the oven. Bake for 35 minutes. Remove and cover the top with sliced tomatoes. Place back into oven for a further 20 minutes. Serve with remainder of sauce, garnished with chopped parsley.

. . . .

DAY NINETEEN

ON RISING: Lemon juice (⅓ cup) and ⅔ cup warm water or 1 cup dandelion coffee

BREAKFAST: Bowl of prunes; fruit toast with jam or honey

10.00 A.M.: Carrot juice

11.00 A.M.: Fresh green juice

12.00 NOON: Carrot, celery and beet-root juice

LUNCH: Focaccia with sundried toma-toes and olives; little coleslaw

2.30 P.M.: Carrot and celery juice

4.00 P.M.: Fruit of choice (2 pieces)

5.30 P.M.: Green tea

DINNER: Buckwheat loaf; brussel sprouts in tomato sauce; scallop potatoes

Coleslaw (serves 2)

2 cups finely shredded cabbage
½ cup grated carrot
½ cup chopped red capsicum
½ cup chopped celery
¼ cup French dressing
¼ cup soy mayonnaise
¼ cup chopped parsley

Preparation: 15 min

Mix all ingredients gently together.

Buckwheat loaf

1 cup buckwheat kernels rinsed
2 slices wheat bread, toasted and crumbed
1½ cups chopped mushrooms
1 tbs egg replacer or 1 egg
1 cup diced onions
1 cup chopped red capsicum
1 tbs tamari
4 tbs water
2 cups water extra
1 tsp basil
dash cayene
½ tsp sage
2 large garlic cloves, chopped
2 tbs lemon juice
1 tbs miso

Preparation: 45 min
Cook: 30–40 min

Buckwheat kernels are featured in this savoury mock meat loaf. Hearty and satisfying, this loaf makes fine leftovers to use in sandwiches. Bring the 2 cups water to a boil in a small pot. Add the buckwheat, stir and cook for 15–20 minutes. Drain any remaining water from the buckwheat. Put half buckwheat aside in a medium bowl, the other half in a food processor. Add bread crumbs, spices and the egg to the food processor and pulse chop until it sticks together. Transfer into the bowl with the rest of the cooked buckwheat. In a separate pan, saute onions, mushrooms, peppers in the lemon juice, bouillon (or tamari) and 4 tbs water. Add miso and garlic after 5 minutes. Stir well, then stir it into the buckwheat until evenly blended. Put into a lightly oiled loaf pan. Bake for 30–40 minutes at 200°. Let stand 10 minutes and turn out. Top with tomato sauce, or serve with a gravy or sauce of your choice. Makes one loaf (8 slices).

Brussels sprouts in tomato sauce

Brussels sprouts

Trim required number of sprouts. Cut each in four quarters and place in casserole dish. Cover with tomato sauce (from recipe on day 12). Cook in the oven at the same time as buckwheat loaf. Approximately 30–40 minutes.

Scallop potatoes

potatoes
1 tsp mixed herbs
1 cup soy milk
½ cup water
1 tsp chopped garlic

Preparation: 10 min
Cook: 1 hr

Scrub and thinly slice required amount of potatoes. Lay in a casserole dish. Mix other ingredients together and pour over potatoes. Cover pan and cook 30–40 minutes.

. . . .

DAY TWENTY

ON RISING: Lemon juice (⅓ cup) and ⅔ cup warm water or 1 cup dandelion coffee

BREAKFAST: Porridge with soy or oat milk

10.00 A.M.: Carrot juice

11.00 A.M.: Fresh green juice and 1 tsp barley green powder

12.00 NOON: Carrot, celery and beet-root juice

LUNCH: Plate of mixed salad; include bean sprouts; 2 slices bread or 1 roll

2.30 P.M.: Carrot and celery juice

4.00 P.M.: Scones with unsugared jam

5.30 P.M.: Green tea

DINNER: Pasta with curried cauliflower sauce; salad

Curried cauliflower sauce with pasta

1 medium thinly sliced onion
1 small sliced red capsicum
1 tsp cumin seeds
3 tsp curry powder
1 tbs plain wholemeal flour
2½ cups soy milk
500 g chopped and cooked cauliflower
300 g pasta of your choice
½ cup toasted almonds

Saute onions in a little water till soft, add capsicum, cumin seeds, curry powder and flour. Gradually stir in soy milk and water, bring to boil and stir till thickened. Add cauliflower. Cook pasta in boiling water, drain. Serve cauliflower mixture over pasta, and sprinkle with chopped almonds.

Scones

2 cups wholemeal flour
1 cup soy milk (more if necessary)

4 tsp salt skip
½ tsp herbamare seasoning

For fruit scones

1 cup dried fruit of choice
1 tbs cinnamon
1 tbs honey
1 tbs mixed spice

Sieve flour, salt skip and ¼ tsp herba-mare. Add soy milk. Mix to a soft dough, knead lightly, then pat out and cut into scone rounds. Bake in moderate oven approximately 20 minutes. Dried fruit added will make sweet scones. Add herbs to basic mix to make savoury.

Perishables for week four

Bread Loaf — ½
Butter — 2 oz
Cannelloni — 1 pkt
Chick Peas — 375 g
Eggs — 6
Filo Pastry Slices — 6
Fruit Bread Loaf — ¼
Pita Bread — 2
Rice Pasta Spirals — 250 g
Rolls — 4
Sorj Bread — 2 sheets
Soy Milk — 2 ltr.
Tofu—block — 600 g approx.
Yoghurt — 300–400 ml
Alfalfa—punnet — 1

Asparagus Spears — 20
Avocado — 3
Bananas — 4
Beetroot — 5
Broccoli—head — 1
Carrots — 10 kg
Cauliflower — 1
Celery—bunch — 2
Corn on Cob — 4
Fruit Pieces — 6–8
Golden Nugget Pumpkin — 1
Green Capsicum — 1
Lemons — 8
Lettuce — 5
Mung Beans — 100 g
Mushrooms — 200 g
Onions — 6
Parsley—bunch — 1
Parsnip — 4
Pears — 4–5
Potatoes — 2 kg
Pumpkin — 1 kg
Radish—bunch — 1
Red Capsicum — 1
Silverbeet—leaves — 4
Snow Peas — ¼ kg
Spinach—bunch — 4
Spring Onions—bunch — 1
Sprouts—punnet — 1
Sweet Potato — 1
Tomatoes — 12

. . . .

DAY TWENTY-ONE

ON RISING: Lemon juice (⅓ cup) and

⅔ cup warm water or 1 cup dandelion coffee

BREAKFAST: Half canteloupe or ½ grapefruit or 2 pieces of fruit

10.00 A.M.: Carrot juice

11.00 A.M.: Fresh green juice and 1 tsp barley green powder

12.00 NOON: Carrot, celery and beetroot juice

LUNCH: Split pea soup; wholemeal or rye toast

2.30 P.M.: Carrot juice with celery or parsley juice

4.00 P.M.: Melons or grapes on their own or other fruit

5.30 P.M.: Green tea

DINNER: Potato pancake; baked parsnips and sweet potato; green beans

Split pea soup (serves 2)

2 cups yellow split peas
6 cups water
½ chopped onion
2 stalks celery chopped
1 tsp cumin powder
1 tbs Jensens vegetable seasoning
½ tsp chopped garlic

Cook all together for approximately one hour or until peas are very soft. You may need to add more water. Bamix or puree in a food processor, serve with chopped parsley and spring onion on top.

Potato pancake (serves 2–3)

3 medium potatoes, scrubbed
1 zucchini
1 onion
1 egg
1 tsp mixed herbs
2 tbs rice flour
½ tsp herbamare

Grate the vegetables and let stand for 10–15 minutes. Squeeze out the moisture through a sieve. Add the herbs, egg, flour and herbamare. Mix well. Grease a stainless steel frying pan with unsalted butter, heat and add the potato mix, cook gently for 15–20 minutes. Turn pancake over and cook on other side for another 15 minutes. Can be baked in the oven for ¾ hour instead.

. . . .

DAY TWENTY-TWO

ON RISING: Lemon juice (⅓ cup) and ⅔ cup warm water or 1 cup dandelion coffee

BREAKFAST: Porridge with soy or oat milk; currants

10.00 A.M.: Carrot juice

11.00 A.M.: Fresh green juice and 1 tsp barley green powder

12.00 NOON: Carrot, celery and beetroot juice

LUNCH: Salad roll with hommos, corn chowder soup

2.30 P.M.: Carrot and celery juice

4.00 P.M.: Smoothie or fruit

5.30 P.M.: Green tea or a juice

DINNER: Steamed vegetables with sweet and sour tofu

Sweet and sour tempeh or tofu (serves 2)

½ block tempeh or tofu cut in 1.5 cm cubes (200 gm approx.)
1 cup thinly sliced carrots
½ cup mirin (on p. 105 condiments, dips, sauces)
2 red capsicums cut in 1 cm pieces
1 tsp freshly grated ginger
2 tbs tamari sauce and 2 tbs water

Preparation: 20 min
Cook: 20 min

Marinade the tofu or tempeh in the tamari and ginger, then heat in the oven or on top of the stove until thoroughly warmed through. Meanwhile steam capsicums and carrots till just tender. Drain any excess tamari and ginger from the tofu, add tofu to the vegetables and the heated mirin. Serve on a bed of rice or noodles.

. . . .

DAY TWENTY-THREE

ON RISING: Lemon juice (⅓ cup) and ⅔ cup warm water or 1 cup dandelion coffee

BREAKFAST: Wholegrain or rye toast (2–3 slices) with jam, honey or miso

10.00 A.M.: Carrot juice

11.00 A.M.: Fresh green juice and 1 tsp barley green powder

12.00 NOON: Carrot, celery and beetroot juice

LUNCH: Half avocado with dressing; lettuce, beetroot and sprouts; wholewheat or rye bread

2.30 P.M.: Carrot juice

4.00 P.M.: Bowl of dried fruits and soaked almonds

5.30 P.M.: Green tea

DINNER: Sweet potato roulade with tomato sauce; potato chips; salad

Sweet potato roulade (serves 4)

1 tbs butter
$\frac{1}{2}$ cup finely chopped spring onion
2 tbs plain wholemeal flour
1 tsp herbamare
2 tbs water
1$\frac{1}{2}$ cups grated uncooked sweet potato
4 eggs, separated

Preparation: 40 mins
Cook: 15 mins

Roulade
Heat oven to 220°. Saute onion in the butter and water for a few minutes. Add sweet potato and cook, stirring constantly until soft. Stir in flour and allow to cool. Line a swiss roll tin with greased greaseproof paper. Add egg yolks to cool sweet potato mixture. Beat egg whites until stiff peaks form and then fold gently into the sweet potato mix adding the herbamare. Spread the batter into the tin and cook for approximately 12–15 minutes.

Filling
1$\frac{1}{2}$ cups cooked brown rice
2 avocado, roughly mashed
1 cup creamed corn kernels
$\frac{1}{2}$ cup soy mayonnaise

$\frac{1}{4}$ cup finely chopped spring onion

Mix all ingredients together gently. Turn roulade out of tin on to a clean tea-towel, peel paper off the underneath and then spread roulade with the rice mixture and gently roll up as in swiss jam roll. Serve warm or cold.

Potato chips

Scrub required amount of potatoes. Cut into fat wedges. Place skin side down on a greased oven tray. Cover with another tray or greased greaseproof paper. Put in moderate oven. Let steam till nearly cooked. Remove cover and increase oven heat to allow wedges to crisp and brown. Sprinkle with herbamare if liked or brush with tamari before crisping.

. . . .

DAY TWENTY-FOUR

ON RISING: Lemon juice ($\frac{1}{3}$ cup) and $\frac{2}{3}$ cup warm water or 1 cup dandelion 'coffee'

BREAKFAST: Stewed pears or apples; yoghurt and oil mix

10.00 A.M.: Carrot juice

11.00 A.M.: Fresh green juice and 1 tsp barley green powder

95

12.00 NOON: Carrot, celery and beet-root juice

LUNCH: Tofu millet salad; lettuce and tomato

2.30 P.M.: Carrot and celery juice

4.00 P.M.: Almonds (½ cup) and ½ cup of dates

5.30 P.M.: Green tea

DINNER: Stuffed golden nugget pumpkin; cauliflower with white sauce

Stuffed golden nuggets (pumpkin)

1 golden nugget pumpkin (if small, allow 1 per person and double stuffing mix.)
½ cup wholemeal bread crumbs
1 dsp finely chopped capsicum
1 dsp finely chopped celery
1 dsp finely chopped spring onion
1 dsp finely chopped parsley
1 tsp finely grated lemon rind
pinch mixed herbs
shake of herbamare
½ cup cooked brown rice

Preparation: 30 min
Cook: 30 min

Cut pumpkin in half, scoop out seeds. Place in baking dish and cover with another dish and bake in a moderate oven until pumpkin is nearly cooked, approximately ½ hour. While pumpkin is baking, mix together all other ingredients. Remove pumpkin from oven, fill cavities with stuffing. Replace in oven for 15–20 minutes. Serve with cauliflower and broccoli and mustard flavoured white sauce.

White sauce

1 cup soy milk
½ cup water
1 small onion
1 tbs soy mayonnaise
1 tsp hot English mustard
1 tsp yeast flakes
¼ tsp herbamare to taste
1 dsp corn flour (mixed with enough water to dissolve)

Preparation: 10 min
Cook: 10 min

Dice onions, boil in water. When clear add soy milk, herbamare, mustard and bouillon. Bring back to boil, thicken with corn flour and let boil again for one minute. Then whisk through the soy mayonnaise and serve. Goes well with chick pea dishes, cauliflower crepes and oven steamed or baked vegetables.

DAY TWENTY-FIVE

ON RISING: Lemon juice (⅓ cup) and ⅔ cup warm water or 1 cup dandelion 'coffee'

BREAKFAST: Porridge with soy milk; currants

10.00 A.M.: Carrot juice

11.00 A.M.: Miso soup with nori; bread

12.00 NOON: Carrot, celery and beetroot juice

LUNCH: Plate of mixed salad greens; dressing; mountain bread or sorj bread

2.30 P.M.: Carrot juice

4.00 P.M.: Fruit (2 pieces)

5.30 P.M.: Green tea

DINNER: Oriental pasta

Oriental pasta (serves 2)

125 g pack rice pasta spirals—cooked till al dente and strained
4–6 mushrooms sliced (shiitake if possible, they need to be soaked in filtered water for 30 mins, then stalks removed)
½ cup julienne carrots
½ red capsicum sliced thinly
½ onion cut in wedges
2 tbs lemon juice
½ tbs each honey, mirin and grated ginger root
½ cup julienne parsnips
½ cup diced cabbage
1 tbs each of tamari and water
dash cayenne
1 clove garlic crushed and extra tamari to taste

Preparation: 30 min
Cook: 10 min

Steam all vegetables except mushrooms. Cook mushrooms in tamari and water for about 10 minutes and strain. Mix them with steamed vegetables and pasta. Stir together mirin, honey, ginger, cayenne, lemon juice, garlic and tamari. Pour over pasta and vegetables. Can be served hot or cold.

DAY TWENTY-SIX

ON RISING: Lemon juice (⅓ cup) and ⅔ cup warm water or 1 cup dandelion 'coffee'

BREAKFAST: Muesli with soy or oat milk

10.00 A.M.: Carrot juice

11.00 A.M.: Fresh green juice and 1 tsp barley green powder

12.00 NOON: Carrot, celery and beetroot juice

LUNCH: Corn on the cob or asparagus with wholemeal roll

2.30 P.M.: Carrot juice

4.00 P.M.: Melons or grapes or 2 pieces of fruit

5.30 P.M.: Green tea

DINNER: Vegetable pie with mashed potato

Vegetable pie with mashed potato (serves 2–3)

1 cup diced onion
1 cup diced carrot
1 cup brown lentils
½ cup wholemeal plain flour or rice flour
1 cup tomato puree
1 kilo potatoes (cooked and mashed)
1 cup diced pumpkin
1 cup diced parsnip
1 tsp chopped garlic
1 tbs tamari or soy sauce to taste
1 tbs curry powder

Preparation: 35 min
Cook: 40 min

Place 4 cups water in saucepan with 1 cup lentils and bring to boil, simmer for 30 minutes. When cooked, drain off excess water. Lightly steam carrot, onion, pumpkin and parsnip. Mix all ingredients together, except potato. Grease casserole with unsalted butter. Put mixture into casserole dish. Top with mashed potato. Bake in moderately hot oven until brown (approximately 30–40 minutes). Suggested sauce: tomato, onion and basil (page 107).

. . . .

DAY TWENTY-SEVEN

ON RISING: Lemon juice (⅓ cup) and ⅔ cup warm water and 1 cup dandelion 'coffee'

BREAKFAST: Fruit (2–3 pieces) and almonds

10.00 A.M.: Carrot juice

11.00 A.M.: Fresh green juice and 1 tsp barley green powder

12.00 NOON: Carrot, celery and beetroot juice

LUNCH: Parsnip soup; toasted rye or wholemeal bread

2.30 P.M.: Carrot juice

4.00 P.M.: Smoothie

5.30 P.M.: Green tea

DINNER: Spanikopita with mushroom sauce; brown rice

Parsnip soup (serves 2)

2 medium parsnips chopped
½ onion chopped
3 cups water
pinch herbamare
½ cup soy milk

Preparation: 10 min
Cook: 20 min

Cover and cook all together (except soy milk) till parsnips tender, about 20 minutes. Bamix or food process till smooth. Add ½ cup soy milk and reheat without boiling. Serve with a pinch of nutmeg on top.

Spanikopita (serves 2–3)

1 bunch cooked chopped spinach
1 bunch cooked chopped silverbeet
2 diced sauteed onions
1 cup crumbled tofu
wholemeal filo pastry—6 sheets
1 tbs garlic
1 tsp herbamare
½ cup white sauce
½ dsp oregano
2 tbs lemon juice

1 tsp tamari

Mix all ingredients except pastry. Put about ½ cup spinach mixture on to filo pastry, each sheet being folded in half lengthways. Fold filling in, forming a triangle. Put on greased oven tray, cook in moderate oven until browned and heated through. Suggested sauce: mushroom.

Mushroom sauce

200 g sliced mushrooms
2 tbs tamari
1 clove garlic chopped
2 small sliced onions
1 cup water

Simmer until tender and thicken with cornflour if necessary.

. . . .

DAY TWENTY-EIGHT

ON RISING: Lemon juice (⅓ cup) and ⅔ cup warm water or 1 cup dandelion 'coffee'

BREAKFAST: Toasted fruit bread with unsugared jams or honey

10.00 A.M.: Carrot juice

11.00 A.M.: Fresh green juice and 1 tsp barley green powder

12.00 NOON: Carrot, celery and beet-root juice

LUNCH: Pizza on wholemeal pita bread; green salad

2.30 P.M.: Carrot and celery juice

4.00 P.M.: 1 piece of brownie

5.30 P.M.: Green tea

DINNER: Stuffed cannelloni; mixed steamed vegetables

Stuffed cannelloni

6–8 large cannelloni tubes
1 cup crumbled tofu
1 cup tomato sauce
3 cups diced steamed mixed vegetables of your choice
1 tsp each oregano, thyme, garlic

Sauce
4 cups chopped tomatoes
1 cup stock or water
1½ cups diced carrots
2 tbs chopped parsley
2 cups chopped onions
2 cloves garlic
2 tbs chopped basil

Simmer all sauce ingredients except parsley, together for 20 minutes. Add parsley and blend. Mix crumbled tofu, diced vegies and herbs together and blend with 1 cup of sauce. Fill cannelloni with this mixture and place in a shallow greased baking dish or casserole. Spoon some of the sauce over and cover dish. Bake for approximately 30 minutes at 200°. Heat remaining sauce and pour over pasta, serve with a garnish of chopped parsley.

Brownies

1 tbs egg substitute mixed with 2 tbs water
⅓ cup carob powder
1 tsp vanilla
1 cup wholemeal flour
½ cup honey
1 tsp cinnamon
¼ cup soy mayonnaise
¾ cup almonds chopped

Beat egg substitute and vanilla. Add honey, soy mayonnaise, carob, flour and spices. Stir in nuts, put into greased square pan and bake 25 minutes at 200°C.

Breads

Wholewheat bread (makes two 500 g loaves)

30 g compressed yeast
$\frac{1}{4}$ cup soy flour
2 cups warm water
$4\frac{1}{2}$ cups wholewheat flour
1 tsp herbamare

Beat the yeast and soy flour with $\frac{2}{3}$ cup of the warm water. Leave in a warm place for 5 minutes or until the mixture becomes frothy. Mix most of the flour and herbamare in a large bowl. Pour in the yeast mixture and add the remaining flour. Mix remaining liquid in with a wooden spoon. Draw up the flour with your hands to form a dough, turn out on to a floured surface and knead thoroughly until the dough has a smooth, velvety surface. Put into a clean bowl and leave covered in a warm place for 1 hour to rise. This process is called proving. It also enhances the flavour of the bread. After 1 hour, turn the dough out on to a floured surface, punch your fist into the dough, and knead it again thoroughly for a few minutes. Divide the dough and shape it into two loaves. Put these into two greased loaf pans and leave them to rise again for another 10 minutes before baking. Bake for 15 minutes in preheated oven at 220°C. Reduce temperature to 180°C and bake further 30 minutes.

Sourdough starter

1 cup kibbled rye
1 tsp ground caraway seeds
1 tsp ground fennel seeds
1 tbs raw cane sugar
A little lukewarm buttermilk or soy yoghurt

Mix all the ingredients together to a thick paste. Dust the top with wholemeal flour so that the dough does not dry out too much; cover the bowl with a tea towel and set aside in a warm, draught-free spot. Knead the starter each day, if necessary adding a little lukewarm water. Note the leavening process takes 2–3 days.

3 cups wholemeal flour
$1\frac{2}{3}$ cups kibbled rye
$1\frac{1}{2}$ cups lukewarm soy milk
60 g dried yeast
1 tsp raw cane sugar
$\frac{1}{2}$ quantity sourdough starter
2–3 tsp herbamare
1 tsp ground caraway seeds
$\frac{1}{2}$ tsp coriander or poppy seeds

Mix together the flour and rye in a bowl and make a well in the centre. Mix a little of the milk with the yeast and sugar and add this to the flour. Cover the bowl with a tea towel and set aside for about 15 minutes. Add the remaining milk, the sourdough starter, herbamare, caraway and coriander and combine thoroughly, kneading with the hands or an electric mixer. Shape the dough into a loaf and set aside for about 30 minutes. Brush with lukewarm milk and sprinkle with poppy seeds. Bake for about 50 minutes in a pre-heated oven at 220°C. Note: leave a cupful of water in the oven with the bread.

Sourdough bread

Sourdough starter
1 cup rye flour
½ cup soy milk

Mix together and let stand, covered for 2–3 days till sour smelling and bubbly.

14 cups wholewheat flour
5 cups water
1½ tsp sea salt
1 cup sourdough starter

Mix 7 cups flour with water, salt, and starter. Add remaining flour slowly until dough becomes too thick to stir. Knead gently until smooth, uniform, and elastic. Cover and let rise for 2 hours in non-metal bowl. Knead dough again. Shape into 3 or 4 loaves. Cut shallow slits in top to keep from cracking. Place in oiled and floured bread pans. Cover. Let rise 4–6 hours. Place in a cold oven with a pan of plain water on oven floor. Bake at 220°C for 15 minutes. Lower heat to 180°C. Continue cooking until golden, about 45 minutes. Remove from pans to cool. Cut into thin slices before serving. Yields 3–4 loaves.

Corn bread (makes 1 loaf)

1 cup wholewheat pastry flour
1 cup cornmeal or corn flour
1 tbs salt skip
⅛ tsp sea salt
¾ cup soy milk
¼ cup water
¼ cup melted butter
¼ cup pure maple syrup
⅛ tsp vanilla extract

Preheat oven to 180°C. Mix flour, cornmeal, salt skip and salt in a bowl. In a separate bowl, beat soy milk, water, butter, maple syrup and vanilla together using a whisk. Combine wet and dry ingredients. Stir a few times. Do not stir too much or the dough will become tough. Pour into oiled loaf pan and bake at 180° for 45 minutes to 1 hour. Check with a toothpick; when it comes out clean, the bread is done.

Pita Bread

2½ cups atta flour or 1½ cups wholemeal and ¾ cup of unbleached baker's flour
pinch salt
⅓ cup plain yoghurt at room temperature

DIPS AND SPREADS

FROM BOTTOM LEFT: Parsnip pate (page 106), Hommous (page 62), Lima bean
dip (page 104), Guacamole (page 79)

SAVORIES

FROM TOP: Stuffed tomatoes, Stuffed mushrooms, Stuffed celery (page 107)

MIDDLE RIGHT: Tofu rice balls (page 107)

MIDDLE LEFT AT BACK: Pastry vegetable sticks (page 139), Party spanikopita at front (page 99)

FRONT: Club sandwiches (page 107)

DESSERTS

CLOCKWISE FROM TOP: Apple crumble (page 130), Poached pears with carob sauce (page 133), Prune mousse (page 135), Jane's steamed pudding and custard (page 133), Grape jelly (page 133) and Apple jelly (page 133)

CAKES

FROM TOP: Pikelets (page 137), Carob balls (page 67), Muffins (page 136), Chewy double carob chip cookies (page 140)

MIDDLE LEFT: Strawberry cheesecake (page 131)

MIDDLE RIGHT: Banana cake (page 135)

FRONT: Fruit cake (page 86)

warm water to mix

Sift flours, add salt and yoghurt then water. Mix to pliable dough. Knead for 8 minutes. Leave to rest under a dish for $1\frac{1}{2}$–2 hours. Roll, cut into small portions. Roll flat and cook in dry pan. Flatten to release steam and brush lightly with butter or ghee.

Batter bread (makes 2 loaves)

$4\frac{1}{2}$ cups wholemeal flour
1 tbs brown sugar
2 tsp herbamare
1 tbs dried yeast
3 cups warm water

Mix all ingredients together. Beat thoroughly, using the dough hook on the mixer for a few minutes or mix by hand. Preheat oven to just on (yeast is activated at 36–38°C—above 40°C yeast deteriorates and dries). Tins can be warmed while mixing. Place batter into greased tins. Spray with water. Cover with greased greaseproof paper and place in the 'just warm' oven or else place in sink of hot water. It should double in size in 30–45 minutes. Remove paper, turn oven up to 200°C and bake for about 35 minutes. Remove from tins and cool on wire rack.

Variations for Batter Bread

Fruit bread

Add 3 cups dried fruits (currants, sultanas, raisins).

Savoury bread

Add onion flakes, parsley, olives as desired.

Rye bread

Use $\frac{1}{2}$ rye and $\frac{1}{2}$ wholemeal and increase water to just under $3\frac{1}{2}$ cups.

Condiments, dips, sauces

Almond ginger sauce for vegetables (serves 2–3)

$1\frac{1}{2}$ cups almonds with skin on, soaked overnight
2 cups water
1 tbs barley miso
1 tsp garlic
1 tbs grated green ginger
1 tbs tamari
2 tbs lemon juice

Preparation: 10–15 min

Chop almonds roughly then place in food

processor with all other ingredients. Process till smooth. Can be used hot or cold or as a dip.

Avocado gazpacho

3 avocados chopped
1 small red Spanish onion
1 small green capsicum
1 small yellow capsicum
2 cloves crushed garlic
1 cup soy yoghurt
2 cups water
1 tbs chopped fresh coriander
2 tbs lemon juice
$\frac{1}{4}$ tsp sambal oelek
1 tbs apple cider vinegar
2 large tomatoes, scrape out and put aside seeds and pulp
2 tbs chopped fresh basil

Blend or process avocados, lemon juice, garlic, yoghurt, vinegar and sambal oelek until smooth. Stir in basil, coriander, and cover. Refrigerate for 1 hour. Blend onion, peppers, tomato pulp and seeds with water, stir in finely chopped tomato cases. Combine the two mixtures, stir well and chill. Garnish with chopped parsley.

Bean dip

2 cups cooked lima beans
2 tsp chopped garlic
2 tbs lemon juice
100 g silken tofu
$\frac{1}{2}$ tsp sweet paprika
1 tsp honey
2 tsp cumin
2 tbs cider vinegar

Puree beans in food processor. Whiz in remaining ingredients. Can be used as a dip or thinned down with water and used as a sauce on pasta or vegetables.

Cauliflower dip

$\frac{1}{2}$ medium cauliflower, steamed till tender
1 onion chopped
2 cups soy yoghurt
2 cloves garlic crushed
2 tsp ground coriander
1 tsp ground cumin
$\frac{1}{4}$ tsp hot paprika
$\frac{1}{2}$ cup chopped chives

Saute the onion and spices in a little water until onion looks transparent, 3 minutes approximately. Blend all ingredients together until smooth. Can be thinned with a little soy milk and used as a sauce over vegetables.

Mock cheese sauce

3 cups water
$\frac{1}{4}$ cup nutritional yeast flakes
$\frac{1}{4}$ cup rolled oats
2 tbs diced onion
1 clove garlic chopped
$\frac{1}{8}$ tsp turmeric powder

¼ cup arrowroot powder
½ tbs tamari or soy sauce
1 tsp basil or herbs
dash cayenne

Put everything into a blender and blend until very smooth. Pour into a small saucepan and heat on a low heat until boiling. Whisk to remove any lumps.

Green dip

2 cups grated zucchini, discard excess juice
2 tbs mayonnaise
½ avocado
1 tbs chopped spring onion
2 garlic cloves
½ tsp coriander powder
½ green capsicum
½ tsp tamari

Put zucchini in food processor or blender. Blend in rest of ingredients, and chill.

Golden sauce for pasta (2 serves)

1 cup diced carrots
1 cup diced sweet potato
½ cup diced onion
1 cup diced pumpkin
1 tsp crushed garlic
1 tsp herbamare
1 tsp cumin powder

Preparation: 20 min
Cook: 30 min

Place all ingredients in a saucepan and cover with water. Bring to a boil, then simmer gently for approximately 30 minutes. Mash or puree the vegetables and serve over pasta, sprinkle with a little spring onion and just a little fresh, grated parmesan cheese.

Lemon and mustard vinaigrette with garlic

3 tbs fresh lemon juice
1 tsp Dijon mustard
¼ tsp freshly minced garlic
1 tsp dried tarragon leaf
¼ tsp balsamic vinegar

Mix all ingredients well and serve.

Mirin sauce

1¼ cup apple cider vinegar
½ cup honey

Boil together until mixture is reduced and thickened. Bottle and keep for vegetable or other rice dishes.

Nut cheese

1 cup almonds
2 cups filtered water

Soak the almonds in extra water overnight. Rinse and drain away water. Put almonds in a blender. Add the 2 cups filtered water, blend until creamy. Add garlic if liked. Transfer mix into a glass jar, cover and leave in a warm place 6–9 hours till settled into curds. Strain out the soft cheese part on top. Let hang in cheesecoth or similar cloth for a day to allow cheese to firm up.

Parsnip paté (makes 1½ cups)

½ cup sliced parsnips
¼ cup almonds
½ cup millet, cooked
1 tbs minced onion
½ tsp basil
½ tsp herbamare
1 tbs chopped parsley
¼ cup chopped celery
½ tbs water
¾ tbs tamari
½ tbs flax oil

Preparation: 35 min
Cook: 20 min

Cook the parsnips until tender, drain and mash. Whilst parsnips and millet are cooking, grind almonds. Place celery, water, tamari and oil into blender and blend to a pulp. Mix with all the remaining ingredients. Place in a bowl, refrigerate and serve as a dip or spread.

Satay sauce

½ litre vegetable stock or water
1 cup ground almonds
or any nut butter except peanut
½ tsp chopped garlic
1 tsp grated green ginger
1 diced onion
3 tbs kuzu or arrowroot (for thickening)
1 tsp cider vinegar
½ tsp curry powder
¼ tsp hot paprika
1 tsp honey
1 tbs low salt tamari

Saute onion in a little water. Add the rest of the ingredients except thickener. Boil for a few moments. Dissolve thickener in cold water add to other ingredients and boil for 1 minute. Adjust seasonings to taste.

Soy yoghurt dill sauce

½ cup soy yoghurt
2 tbs soy mayonnaise
1 tsp crushed dill
1 tbs lemon juice

Whip together and serve.

Spinach yoghurt and dill

1 cup finely chopped spinach
½ cup soy mayonnnaise
2 cups soy yoghurt

2 tsp kuzu or arrowroot dissolved in cold water
2 tsp powdered dill seed

Gently heat yoghurt and mayonnaise, add dill and thicken with kuzu if needed, add chopped spinach just prior to serving.

Tofu mayonnaise

1 kg tofu—squeeze out excess water
$1/2$ cup tamari
2 cups flax seed oil
1 cup cider vinegar
1 cup lemon juice
$1^1/2$ tbs honey
1 tbs mustard

Blend all ingredients together in food processor. This quantity makes $4^1/2$ large cups.

Tomato onion basil sauce

1 cup tomatoes chopped
1 onion chopped
1 cup water
2 tsp fresh basil or 1 tsp dried basil
1 tsp garlic
1 dsp corn flour mixed with 2 dsp cold water

Cook onion until soft. Add all of the other ingredients. Thicken with corn flour. Boil for one minute. Serve warm.

Savoury finger food

Small tomatoes, celery and snow peas can all be 'stuffed' with a mixture of tofu and any other flavours you wish.
Simply cream the tofu and add whatever you please.
For tomatoes, cut the top off and scoop out the seeds with a teaspoon. Fill the cavity and top with a sprig of parsley.
For celery sticks, wash and dry, pipe on the filling and sprinkle with appropriate seeds. Fill the long sticks then cut into lengths. Much easier to handle this way. Cucumber can be cut in half lengthways, scoop out the seeds and fill, then cut in lengths.

Club sandwiches are a welcome addition. Use several different types of bread, ie rye, wholemeal and dark rye. Make sure your fillings are reasonably moist and will hold together when cut into small pieces. Fillings can be salmon and cucumber, hommous and lettuce and cress, mashed beans and gherkins. Anything that is within the suggested guidelines.

Tofu, Rice and Almond Balls

2 cups cooked brown rice
250 g tofu
$3/4$ cup almonds
3 tbs oat bran
1 tbs onion powder
1 tsp herbamare seasoning

(or other choice)

Place all ingredients in a food processor and pulse chop till evenly distributed and holding together. Roll the mixture into 4cm balls and coat in bran if liked. Bake in fairly hot oven (250°C) for 30 mins, turning once.

Soups

Barley soup (serves 3–4)

$\frac{1}{2}$ cup pearl barley
2 onions
2 potatoes
2 carrots
1 parsnip
1 turnip
1 swede
2 sticks celery
6 cups water
1 tsp each basil, marjoram, oregano
1 tsp garlic
2 tsp Jensens broth
$\frac{1}{4}$ cup chopped parsley
2 bay leaves

Chop vegetables. Cook barley, onions, potatoes, and carrots with bay leaf in water for about 1 hour. Then add remaining ingredients. Cook further $\frac{1}{2}$ hour for best results. Top with parsley and serve with crusty bread or toast.

Cold beet borscht soup (serves 2)

$1\frac{3}{4}$ cups diced raw beetroot
$\frac{1}{2}$ cup diced raw carrot
$\frac{1}{2}$ cup diced cucumber
1 small onion sliced
1 cup diluted beet juice or vegetable broth
2 tbs lemon juice
dash of celery salt
dill to taste
1 tsp vegetable seasoning
sliced cucumber, dill and plain yoghurt to garnish

Preparation: 30 min

Blend first nine ingredients adding more liquid if necessary. Serve cold, garnish with additional slice of cucumber, dill and spoonfuls of yoghurt.

Carrot soup with ginger, lemon and fresh coriander (serves 2)

$1\frac{1}{2}$ cups roughly chopped onion
3 cups chopped carrot
1 tbs freshly grated ginger
1 tbs chopped fresh coriander or 1 tsp dried coriander
2 cups water (plus extra $\frac{1}{2}$ cup water)
$\frac{1}{2}$ cup lemon juice
1 tbs honey

Preparation: 30 min

Cook the onions in the ½ cup water, adding the carrots when the onions are cooked. Add the ginger and water, cover. When the carrots are soft, puree soup, add lemon juice and honey. Garnish with fresh coriander.

Cauliflower soup (serves 2)

2 cups roughly chopped cauliflower
2 tbs diced onions
¼ cup soy milk
¼ tsp cumin powder
½ tsp coriander

Preparation: 5 min
Cook: 20 min

Cook onion and cauliflower in enough water to cover well, cook until soft. Blend and add cumin, soy milk and more water if necessary. Simmer 5 minutes, garnish with chopped parsley and serve.

Chunky vegetable soup (serves 2)

½ onion chopped
¼ cup scrubbed and diced carrot
¼ cup diced pumpkin
¼ cup diced celery
¼ tsp basil
¼ cup diced snow peas
¼ cup diced zucchini
¼ cup diced broccoli
1 bay leaf
3 cups water

Preparation: 20 min
Cook: 30 min

Bring all to boil and simmer gently for 30 minutes. Serve with wholemeal bread rolls.

Corn and red pepper chowder (serves 2)

½ cup tofu
2 cups water
1 tbs arrowroot powder
1 dsp onion powder
½ cup red capsicum, diced small
¼ tsp crushed garlic
¼ tsp dried thyme
1½ cups corn kernels
1 dsp tamari
½ chopped onion
¼ tsp sea salt

Preparation: 20 min
Cook: 15 min

Place 1 cup water and tofu into a blender and puree. Add the arrowroot and onion powder, garlic and thyme and process for a few minutes. Place chopped onion in a pan and add the extra ¼ cup water. Saute for a few minutes, add red capsicum, corn and sea salt. Simmer for 10 minutes, stir in tofu mix, reheat and simmer for 2 minutes. Add extra water if soup is too thick. Serve with crispy bread for a satisfying meal.

Lentil soup (serves 3)

1 cup red or green lentils
1 medium onion sliced
1 carrot sliced
1 celery stick sliced
1 dsp cider vinegar
1 clove garlic crushed
1 tbs tomato puree
8 cups hot water
1 tsp herbamare

Preparation: 15 min
Cook: 1 hour

Wash lentils and place all ingredients except vinegar in a pan. Bring to boil, cover and simmer for about 1 hour. Add more water if needed. Stir occasionally. When all vegetables are cooked add vinegar and serve.

Lentil and vegetable soup (serves 2)

1 tbs water
½ onion chopped
½ clove garlic crushed
¼ cup chopped celery
¼ cup carrot peeled and chopped
¼ cup red lentils
sea salt
3 cups stock

Preparation: 15 min
Cook: 40 min

Heat the water and saute the onion and garlic until soft. Add the remaining ingredients and simmer gently for 40 minutes until the lentils and vegetables are tender. Adjust the seasoning to taste and serve with crusty wholemeal bread.

Rosy vegetable soup (serves 3)

4 cups stock or water
¾ cup chopped red potatoes
½ cup chopped beetroot
¾ cup of chopped celery
½ cup of chopped silver beet or spinach
½ red onion sliced
1 tsp chopped fresh basil
1 clove garlic crushed and chopped
1 tbs uncooked rice, barley or other grain
1 tsp tamari
1 tsp lemon juice
¼ tsp coriander
¼ tsp cumin
¼ tsp onion powder
¼ tsp of dill

Preparation: 20 min
Cook: 1 hr 15 min

Bring stock to boil, add washed barley, cover and simmer for 15 minutes. Add vegetables to pot along with spices. Simmer for an hour or so.

Russian borscht soup (serves 3–4)

1½ cups thinly sliced potatoes
4 cups water
1 small carrot thinly sliced
1½ cups chopped onions
1½ tbs cider vinegar
3 cups shredded cabbage
¾ cup thinly sliced beetroot
1 stalk celery chopped
1 cup tomato puree
1 tsp dill
1 tbs honey

Place all vegetables in pot, add the water, and cook till tender, approximately 30 minutes. Add the seasonings and simmer another 15 minutes. Serve hot, topped with soy yoghurt (optional) and dill leaf.

Silverbeet soup (serves 2)

2 cups chopped silverbeet
½ onion, chopped
1¼ cups water
1 tbs Jensens broth
⅓ tsp nutmeg
pinch herbamare
½ cup soy milk

Preparation: 10 min
Cook: 25–30 min

Saute onions in a little water for about 5 minutes with lid on the pan. Add silverbeet, put lid back on and simmer another 5 minutes. Add water and bring to boil, then simmer gently for 15–20 minutes. Remove from heat and puree with Bamix or food processor. Add soy milk and nutmeg. Reheat carefully but do not boil. Serve with a sprinkle of chopped dry roasted almonds on top.

Chick pea soup (serves 2–3)

1½ cups dry chick peas
1 cup chopped onions
6 cups water
4 cloves chopped garlic
1 cup water
1 cup finely diced celery
6 bay leaves
1 tsp vegetable salt
2 tbs freshly chopped basil
⅛ tsp crushed saffron (about 10 threads)
1 cup tomato puree

Rinse the chick peas, then soak over-night in water. Cook them in 6 cups of water in a separate pot with the bay leaves for 1½ hours, or until soft. While the chick peas are cooking, braise the onions and celery in the extra cup of water until the onion is softened. Mix the saffron into the onion and celery. Add the tomato puree and let simmer for about 30 minutes. When the chick peas are done, drain them. Add the chick peas to the onion, celery, saffron and tomato mixture. Then add the garlic. Simmer this mixture for about 15 to 20 minutes. If a thinner consistency is desired, add some stock or water. Garnish with basil.

Sprout soup (serves 2)

½ onion, chopped
1 stick celery, sliced
2½ cups water
½ cup mung bean sprouts
½ carrot cut into thin sticks
2 mushrooms, sliced
1 flat tsp barley miso

In a saucepan boil the onion, carrot, celery and water for 10 minutes. Add mung bean sprouts and mushrooms. Boil 3 minutes, take off heat and stir in the miso. Serve.

Sweet potato soup (serves 2)

1½ cups diced sweet potato
1 cup water
1 small leek cleaned and sliced
1 clove garlic
1 tsp lemon juice
1 dsp yeast flakes
¾ cup soy milk

Preparation: 15 min
Cook: 15 min

Place all ingredients except soy milk in a pan and bring to boil. Turn down and simmer covered for 15 minutes or until vegetables are soft. Puree soup and add soy milk. Reheat and serve

with a dollop of yoghurt and garnish of spring onions.

Tomato soup (serve 2)

4 ripe tomatoes
1 cup water
¼ cup chopped onions
⅓ tsp herbamare
1 tsp chopped basil
1 bay leaf
½ tsp honey
¼ cup soy milk (optional)

Preparation: 15 min
Cook: 15 min

Chop tomatoes and onion, put in saucepan with other ingredients except soy milk. Simmer until vegetables are cooked and mushy. Puree and add soy milk if a creamy soup is required or more water if a thinner soup is required.

Vital broth (neutralises acid conditions)

2 cups chopped carrot tops
2 cups chopped celery stalks
2 cups chopped celery leaves
2 cups chopped beetroot leaves
1.25 litres water
2 cups 1 cm thick potato 'peels'
½ cup chopped onion
1 tsp herbamare

Peel potato thickly, most nutrients are in

the skin, cook the thick skins. Combine all ingredients in a pot. Simmer for about 30 minutes, strain and serve liquid.

Pasta dishes

(Pastas are a processed food so use sparingly)

Chinese vegetables with noodles
(serves 2)

8 snow peas
$\frac{1}{2}$ cup stringless green beans
$\frac{1}{2}$ cup capsicum strips
$\frac{1}{2}$ cup carrot strips
2 tsp grated ginger
2 tsp tamari
$\frac{1}{4}$ cup water
2 cups cooked noodles of choice

Preparation: 15 min
Cook: 20 min

Place all ingredients, except noodles in a preheated pan or wok. Saute for 3 minutes. Arrange noodles on 2 serving plates and top with the vegetables. Note any vegetables of your choice can be used to make this nutritious dish.

Curried pasta salad

1 cup brown rice or 2 cups of pasta of choice
4 sliced radishes
1 large bunch finely chopped spring onion

$\frac{1}{4}$ cup soy mayonnaise, thinned with 1 tbs soy milk
curry powder as desired
1 chopped tomato
$\frac{1}{2}$ tsp chopped garlic

Preparation: 20 min
Cook: 15 min

Cook pasta or rice, rinse and cool. Add other ingredients, fold gently through.

Minty pasta

Moulds
1 cup (190 g) Stellini pasta
$\frac{2}{3}$ cup (80 g) peas
$\frac{2}{3}$ cup (70 g) sliced green beans
$\frac{1}{4}$ cup shredded fresh mint
2 tbs chopped fresh chives

Salad
1 red oak leaf lettuce
$\frac{1}{2}$ medium red capsicum, sliced
100 g snow pea sprouts
1 small green cucumber, chopped

Grease 6 moulds (125 ml capacity). Add pasta to large pan of boiling water. Boil, uncovered, until just tender. Drain (do not rinse). Boil or steam beans and peas until just tender; drain. Combine hot pasta, beans, peas and remaining ingredients in bowl. Divide mixture evenly between prepared moulds. Press mixture firmly into moulds. Stand 5 minutes before turning on to plates. If no appropriate mould, press mix into any desired bowl or cup and turn out.

Serve with salad. For salad, combine torn lettuce and remaining ingredients in bowl.

Minted pasta with tomato dressing

2 cups cooked pasta
¾ cup cooked peas
⅓ cup chopped mint
⅓ cup chopped chives

Preparation: 15 min
Cook: 15 min

Mix ingredients together. Press into moulds or a cup and turn out onto a plate of salad greens and pour dressing over.

Tomato dressing

4 medium tomatoes chopped small
2 tbs cider vinegar
¼ flax seed oil
¼ tsp mustard
1 tsp honey

Puree ingredients together.

Vegetable dishes

Baked beans (serves 2)

1 cup lima beans
3 medium tomatoes chopped

2 onions chopped
2 tbs chopped parsley
1 tsp dried basil
1 tsp herbamare
½ cup water extra
1 cup seasoned bread crumbs

Preparation: 35 min
Cook: 40 min

Soak beans overnight in water with a strip of kombu. Drain beans. Discard soak water. Place in saucepan and cover well with fresh water. Bring to boil and turn down to simmer for 30 minutes. Saute onions in 2 tablespoons water. Add tomatoes, basil, cover and cook gently for 5 minutes. Strain cooking water off beans. Place them in a casserole dish. Pour over the tomato sauce mixture. Sprinkle with bread crumbs and bake uncovered in a moderate oven for 30–40 minutes. Sprinkle with parsley when serving.

Bean and olive bake

1 cup beans, lima, haricot or a mixture, soak overnight
1 cup pureed tomatoes
1 small onion chopped
1 tsp garam masala
½ tsp ground cumin
¼ tsp chilli
1 tsp barley miso
¼ tsp herbamare
¼ cup rye or barley flakes

1 tbs chopped black olives
¼ cup rice
1 dsp chopped parsley

Preparation: 30 min
Cook: 45 min

Drain the beans and cover with fresh water and bring to the boil. Cook till soft then drain and mash. To cook rice, boil fast for 10 minutes, cover and simmer for 25–35 minutes. Heat half cup water in a pan and gently cook the onion until just soft. Add the spices and cook for another 30 seconds. Add tomatoes and cook for five minutes then remove mixture from the heat and stir in the rye flakes, rice, olives. Add the beans, miso and herbamare. Spoon the mixture into a lightly greased, 20 × 10 cm loaf pan and bake in a preheated oven at 190° for 20–30 min. Turn out and garnish with black olives and parsley. Serve hot.
Suggested sauce: Tomato, onion and basil sauce or Onion gravy.

Cauliflower baskets with capsicum sauce

8 sheets filo pastry or use wholemeal sorj bread instead of pastry

Cut pastry in half, cut each half into four pieces. Layer four pieces together, unevenly overlapping. Press into prepared tins. Bake in moderate oven about 15 minutes or until well browned. Cool pastry in tins. Spoon filling evenly into pastry cups, serve with red capsicum sauce.

Filling

500 g cauliflower
⅓ cup (80ml) vegetable stock
1 medium red Spanish onion, thinly sliced
½ bunch (325 g) English spinach

Cut cauliflower into flowerets, cook onion, stirring, until soft. Add cauliflower and stock, simmer, covered, about 4 minutes or until cauliflower is just tender. Add spinach, stir until just wilted.

Capsicum sauce

3 medium red capsicums
2 tbs cider vinegar
1 clove garlic, crushed
1 tbs oil (olive)

Quarter capsicums, remove seeds and membranes. Grill peppers, skin side up, until skin blisters and blackens. Peel away skin. Blend or process peppers, garlic, vinegar and oil until smooth. Place sauce in small pan, stir over heat until hot.

Creamed Brussels sprouts

2 cups small Brussels sprouts
½ cup yoghurt
¼ cup finely diced onion
¼ cup finely diced capsicum

Preparation: 20 min
Cook: 15 min

Steam sprouts and toss with other ingredients. Can also serve carrots, broccoli, and beans with same sauce.

Bean and vegetable stew

500 g assorted dry beans
2 cups vegetable stock or water
½ cup diced carrots
1 tsp garlic powder or
3 cloves fresh garlic
⅓ cup vegetable stock or water
½ cup diced celery
½ cup diced parsnips
1 cup cooked rice or pasta
1 onion diced
½ cup sliced mushrooms
1 tsp dried parsley
1 bay leaf
⅓ cup tamari
1 tsp dried basil

Rinse the beans, then soak overnight in water. Drain, cover with fresh water and cook. Drain any excess away and place beans in a pot. Cover with vegetable stock or water; the amount added depends on whether you want a soup or stew. Add the vegetables, tamari, herbs and spices. Cook until carrots and parsnips are tender, add the rice or pasta and heat through.

Millet burgers

1½ cups hulled millet
1 carrot grated finely
1 onion, grated
3 tbs almonds, ground
½ cup whole grain bread crumbs
1 clove garlic, chopped
1 tbs tamari
¼ tsp thyme or marjoram
½ tsp sage
4 cups water

Bring 4 cups water to boil, add millet and stir occasionally. Simmer for 30 minutes and drain. Lightly saute carrot, garlic and onion in ¼ cup water. Then cover and cook on low heat for 5 minutes. Transfer to a large bowl and mix in millet and other ingredients. Shape into 6 or 8 burgers. If too crumbly, add a litle water until they hold together well. Bake on an oiled baking dish or make a loaf. Enhance the loaf with a well-flavoured gravy. Serve burgers with all the trimmings—tofu mayonnaise, tomato sauce, on wholewheat buns or pita bread.

Mushroom barley pilaf (serves 2)

3/4 cup quartered button mushrooms
3/4 cup barley soaked and cooked
1/4 cup finely chopped spring onions
1/2 tsp chopped garlic
2 tsp lemon juice
1 tsp miso
3/4 cup chopped tomato

Put the barley, mushrooms and spring onions into a bowl. Blend the rest of the ingredients in a blender. Stir the sauce and pilaf together and serve on a platter of baby greens. Garnish with tomato wedges.

Stuffed mushrooms (serves 4)

2–4 mushrooms per person (depending on size). Use the flatter type not small button mushrooms
1 cup fresh bread crumbs
1 tsp dried mixed herbs or
1 tbs fresh chopped herbs
1 chopped spring onion
1/2 cup chopped lightly toasted almonds
1 tsp fresh chopped garlic
1 dsp mineral bouillon
tamari

Mix stuffing ingredients together. The mix will seem a little dry but moisture from the mushrooms will hold mix together. Wipe the mushroom cups clean with wet kitchen paper or a towel. Place stuffing mix in the cups after trimming

away the stalk, you can add the chopped stalks to the mix. Place the mushrooms on a slightly greased tray or dish and cook for 15 minutes in a moderate oven.

Raw nut loaf

4 cups grated carrots
3 spring onions
5 cloves garlic (1 tbs)
1 cup soaked almonds or hazelnuts
1 dsp miso
1 tsp oregano
1/4 cup chopped fresh parsley
1 tsp curry powder

Chop all ingredients in a food processor. Switch on and off until a mealy (resembling bread crumbs) consistency is achieved. Place in a greased loaf dish, pack down. Refrigerate for several hours and turn out on to a platter.

Rice patties

4 cups cooked brown rice or cooked millet (or 50:50) puree
1/2 cooked rice or millet
1/2 cup wholemeal flour
1 tsp each garlic and grated ginger
1 cup grated carrot
4 chopped spring onions
2 tbs tamari mixed with 2 tbs water
tsp herb salt

Mix all ingredients together and shape into patties. Dry bake in oven 200° on a lightly greased tray, for approximately 30 minutes.

Nori rolls (serves 2)

4 sheets toasted nori
1 avocado peeled and sliced
2 tomatoes sliced
2 cups alfalfa sprouts
2 tbs soy mayonnaise mixed with 4 tbs French dressing

Place 1 sheet nori on a sushi mat. Lay a quarter of the avocado slices down the centre. Add ¼ of the tomato slices, ½ cup alfalfa, and sprinkle with dressing and roll up. Continue with the rest of the rolls.

Nori taco cones

5 toasted nori sheets
½ punnet of alfalfa sprouts
1 medium carrot
1 medium zucchini
1 celery stalk, diced
1 tbs water
1 tbs grated green ginger
horseradish/ginger paste
½ cup tamari
1 tsp honey

Large dice and lightly steam all vegetables, except alfalfa. Mix ginger, horseradish, honey, tamari and water together to make a sauce. Cut nori sheets in half. Put together as required by rolling nori sheets in a cone, adding vegetables and sprouts, then top with sauce. A bowl of rice and a green salad are good accompaniments.

Polenta with tomato sauce

1 cup polenta
4 cups water or stock
1 clove garlic crushed
1 tsp mixed herbs

Bring 4 cups water to boil, gradually add the polenta to the boiling water or stock, stirring as you add the polenta to prevent lumps from forming. Cook over low heat, stirring frequently for about 10 minutes. The polenta burns easily. It has finished cooking when the mixture is hard to stir and the stirring spoon is able to stand within the polenta. Before it becomes too thick, you may want to add herb salt to taste. Once cooked, transfer the polenta to a baking dish or cookie sheet and smooth out until it is a uniform height about 1 cm thick. Mark into squares and brown gently in a moderate oven for 15 mins. Remove from oven.

Tomato sauce

2 cups chopped tomatoes
½ cup water
2 tbs dried oregano
2 tbs chopped parsley
1 cup chopped onions
2 tbs freshly chopped garlic

118

2 tbs freshly chopped basil

To start the sauce, puree the tomato with a little water. Set aside. Braise the onions in water with the garlic, basil and oregano. When the onions are translucent, add the pureed tomatoes. Cook for approximately 20 mins, stirring frequently, until the sauce is thick. Adjust seasonings. There should be about 1½ cups sauce. Serve the polenta with tomato sauce ladled over the top. Garnish with basil or parsley.

Potato and corn bake (serves 2)

2 cups scrubbed chopped potatoes
¼ cup spring onions or
finely chopped onions
1 small stick celery chopped
½ cup peas or diced beans
½ cup corn kernels
freshly chopped parsley
½ tsp paprika
1 cup mustard white sauce

Preparation: 35 min
Cook: 25 min

Steam potatoes and peas or beans until tender. Mix in all other ingredients except paprika and white sauce. Place in lightly buttered dish. Top with sauce and sprinkle with paprika and bake at 200° for 20 minutes or until light golden brown. Top with extra parsley.

Rice and vegetable sushi

½ pkt toasted nori sheets (cut in half)
10 × 18 cm long strips of carrot
½ cm thick
5 × 18 cm long strips of green capsicum
10 × 18 cm long strips of cucumber
5 × 18 cm long strips of red capsicum
250 g brown rice
2 tbs chopped ginger
1 tbs horseradish
2 cloves garlic chopped
1½ cups chopped mushrooms
½ cup tamari

Cook brown rice until very soft. Do not rinse with water when cooked, just drain away any excess water, add ¾ cup mirin sauce (see p. 000) and stir in well. Spread out on tray and allow to cool. Lightly steam carrots and capsicum. Cook mushrooms in tamari, add garlic, drain off any excess liquid, then puree. Puree ginger and horseradish. Place half pieces of nori on flat surface, three-quarters cover with sticky rice, spread a thin layer of ginger and horseradish then layer of mushrooms, then 1 strip of each vegetable across bottom of nori rice sheet. Roll up and seal, having wet a pastry brush with water and brushed along exposed nori sheet. Cut in 6 pieces and serve with dipping sauce of equal quantities of tamari and water.

Savoury stuffed bread

1 loaf wholemeal or sourdough rye bread

Cut crust from one end of loaf. Scoop out loaf and discard centre. Keep crust. Preheat oven to 200°.

Stuffing

4 cups cooked red lentils drained
1 cup finely chopped parsley
1 cup diced carrot
½ cup diced capsicum
herbamare to taste
1 cup diced onion
2 cloves garlic finely chopped
1 tsp tomato paste
¼ cup water

Combine all ingredients except lentils in a saucepan. Saute for 5 minutes. Then cover with lid and cook gently for a further 5 minutes. Stirring often to prevent sticking. Remove from heat and stir in lentils. Mix thoroughly. Press stuffing into loaf crust, pressing in firmly. Replace end crust and bake on a tray for 30 minutes. Set aside for 10 minutes before cutting. To serve remove crusts from both ends and using a serrated knife cut into 8 thick slices.

Scalloped sweet potato

2 large sweet potatoes (kumara)
1 sliced red onion
1 tsp crushed garlic
½ cup soy milk

Scrub potatoes and slice in 2 cm thick slices. Put in a greased dish and cover with onion and garlic mixed with soy milk. Cover and bake in a moderate oven for ¾ hour.

Taco beans

375 g borlotti beans, soaked overnight
3 onions
1 green capsicum
8 tomatoes
2 tbs mixed herbs
2 tbs cornflour mixed in
½ cup cold water
2 red capsicums
3–4 mushrooms
2 tsp chopped garlic
1 tbs oregano
1 cup water

Drain beans, cover with cold water and boil gently till tender, drain. Chop roughly all vegetables and simmer in 1 cup of water for 5 mins. Add herbs. Put lid on pan, cook about 20 minutes. Add beans to sauce, thicken with corn flour.

Terrine

1 cup pureed cooked pumpkin
1 cup pureed cooked spinach
1 cup pureed cooked beetroot

1 cup pureed cooked cauliflower
4 cups stock, 2 tsp bouillon
4 tbs agar agar or 6 tbs kanten flakes

Boil together stock and agar agar or kanten flakes for 15 minutes. Grease a loaf pan or mould with unsalted butter. Place a decoration of vegetables in bottom of mould. Cover thinly with stock. Divide remaining stock in four. Add one portion to each of the vegetable purees. Place alternate layers of each vegetable mix in mould. Allow to set then turn out and decorate.

Legume dishes

Curried lentils

¼ cup water
2 cups chopped red onions
2 cups lentils, washed
1 tsp cumin powder
1 tsp tamari or soy sauce
1¼ cups cheesy sauce page 104
2 tbs lemon juice
3 garlic cloves, minced
2 tsp curry powder
½ tsp cinnamon
2 cups boiling water
3 cups seeded and chopped tomatoes

This dish is delicious as a side dish, or as a main dish with some rice or couscous.

Heat water and lemon juice in large skillet and saute onions for a couple of minutes. Add garlic and lentils and simmer 3 minutes. Stir in the spices. Add boiling water to skillet, stir and cover. Return to a boil, then turn to low and simmer 25 minutes. Meanwhile prepare Cheesy Sauce (see p. 000) and tomatoes. Stir Cheesy Sauce into lentils, then fold in tomatoes. Place in a casserole dish, cover and bake at 200° for 20–30 minutes, until lentils are soft and everything is hot.

Dhal

1 chopped onion
1 crushed clove garlic
1 tsp coriander
1 tsp curry powder
½ tsp turmeric
¾ cup red lentils
2½–3 cups water
1 tsp herbamare
1 dsp tamari

Preparation: 15 min
Cook: 1 hr

Saute onion and herbs in a little water. Add other ingredients and simmer gently stirring occasionally for about 1 hour. Dhal should be about the consistency of pea soup. Serve with vegetables and grains.

Lentil patties with Yoghurt mint sauce (makes 4)

½ cup red lentils
½ stick celery chopped
1 small carrot chopped
2 cups water
½ tsp ground coriander
2 tbs water
¼ tsp cumin
¼ tsp oregano
1 tbs chopped parsley
1 cup wholemeal bread crumbs
2 tbs wholemeal flour or
extra bread crumbs

Soak lentils overnight if possible. Drain lentils and combine lentils, carrot, celery, water, coriander, and cumin in a pan. Bring to the boil. Turn down and simmer for about 20 minutes till vegetables are cooked. Cool and add parsley and bread crumbs. Shape into 4 patties. Coat with wholemeal flour or bread crumbs. Place on greased tray and bake in a moderate oven for about 30 minutes. Turning once. Serve with yoghurt mint sauce.

Yoghurt mint sauce

¼ cup soy yoghurt
2 tsp chopped fresh mint
2 tsp chopped fresh parsley
1 clove crushed garlic
1 tsp lemon juice

Combine all ingredients well.

Lentil pikelets with mushroom salsa

½ cup brown lentils
½ cup wholemeal flour
½ cup soy yoghurt
1 egg
½ tsp caraway seeds
⅓ tsp herbamare
1 tsp baking powder substitute
1 tbs chopped parsley

Preparation: 15 min
Cook: 40 min

Cook lentils in boiling water until tender, drain. Sift flour and baking powder into a bowl and add beaten egg, yoghurt, lentils and all seasonings. Heat and grease a heavy pan with unsalted butter and drop tablespoons of mix into pan and spread a little. Cook until bubbles rise and turn over and cook other side. Makes 4–5 pikelets.

Mushroom salsa

½ medium red capsicum
½ finely chopped red onion
200g mushrooms, sliced, can use shiitake
½ tsp herbamare
1 dsp fresh thyme leaves

Quarter capsicum, remove seeds and membranes, grill and slice. Saute mushrooms and onion in a little water. Drain away any excess liquid, combine all ingredients. Serve on pikelets, top with soy yoghurt and chopped parsley.

Red lentil patties (makes 8)

2 cups cold cooked red lentils
2 cups cold mashed potato
$1/2$ cup finely diced carrot
$1/2$ cup finely diced onion
$1/4$ cup water
$1/2$ cup fine dry bread crumbs

Preparation: 30 min
Cook: 20 min

Saute carrot and onion with water for 3 minutes. Simmer to reduce liquid to nothing and remove pan from heat. Transfer sauteed vegetables to a mixing bowl and combine with lentils and mashed potato. Shape into 8 patties and coat with bread crumbs. Dry bake till golden both sides and heated through. Serve hot or cold with vegetables or salads.

Hunza pie (serves 2–3)

3 cups cooked brown rice
2 small chopped onions
3 cups chopped cooked silverbeet or spinach
1 tbs crushed coriander seeds
1 tbs tamari
1 tsp garlic
1 cup grated firm tofu
2 tbs water

Preparation: 30 min
Cook: 30–40 min

Saute the onions and coriander seeds in the water. Mix all other ingredients with onions and coriander. Transfer mixture to a pie base of wholemeal flour, sorj bread or filo pastry. Cover top of pie with pastry or bread if liked. Brush with a little egg yolk and sprinkle with poppy seeds. Bake for $1/2$–$3/4$ hour in a moderate oven.

Tofu dishes

Crumbed tofu (serves 3–4)

500 g tofu cut in 3 cm cubes
1 cup tomato juice
$1/4$ cup tamari
$1/2$ cup finely chopped spring onions
2 cups fresh bread crumbs

Mix tomato juice, tamari and spring onion. Marinate tofu cubes for 1 hour in the mixture, drain and coat in bread crumbs. Heat on greased tray in moderate oven.

Spinach tofu loaf

2 cups tofu
$1/3$ cup fine bread crumbs
2 cups chopped cooked spinach
1 cup chopped spring onion
1 tbs grated lemon rind

1 tbs dill powder or chopped seed
2 garlic cloves
dash of cayenne
½ lemon, juiced

Squeeze moisture out of cooked spinach. Stir all ingredients except bread crumbs together and place in a casserole or loaf dish that has been lightly buttered. Sprinkle bread crumbs on top. Bake at 200° for 30 minutes. Allow to settle 15 minutes before turning out. Suggested sauce: soy yoghurt dill sauce.

Tofu curry

375 g block tofu
2 cups fresh peas or
chopped green beans, cooked
2 knobs green ginger
2 medium chopped onions
1 cup shredded spinach
1 tsp turmeric powder
1 tsp cumin
1 tsp cardamon
½ tsp cinnamon
1 tsp garam masala
1 tsp mustard seeds
1 tsp poppy seeds
2 cups water
2 tbs lemon juice
¼ cup tamari and ¼ cup water
mixed together

Cut tofu into 1½ cm cubes, marinate in tamari and water. Put the mustard and poppy seeds in a dry pan and place over gentle heat and shake pan gently for a few moments till mustard seeds pop. Add other seasonings and take off heat. Drain tofu and put aside. Saute onions in the marinade. Add the grated green ginger and heat. Add rest of ingredients, heat through and serve over rice.

Tofu in lettuce (serves 2–3)

6 large lettuce leaves washed
400 g mashed tofu
1 cup finely sliced mushrooms
2 tbs tamari
½ cup sliced spring onions
2 tsp garlic

Mix all ingredients except lettuce leaves. Spread mixture in lettuce leaves and roll up. Serve rolls with tomato, capsicum and olives.

Tofu scramble (serves 2)

1¼ cups mashed firm tofu
¼ cup finely chopped fresh parsley
¼ cup flaked slivered toasted almonds
1 tsp tamari
¼ cup chopped spring onions
1 tbs unsalted butter

Mix together the tofu, parsley, almonds and tamari. Melt the unsalted butter in a pan and stir in the tofu mix. Heat through for 3–4 minutes and scramble. Serve with sauteed onions and mushrooms for a delicious combination or serve with other vegetables, or grain of choice or a wholemeal roll. This is also ideal as a light lunch or evening meal for a quick main course.

Vegetable tofu or tempeh burgers (makes 8)

½ cup grated pumpkin
½ cup grated carrot
½ cup grated parsnip
½ cup cooked rice
1 cup tofu or tempeh crumbled (tempeh must be marinated and cooked first)
1 tsp lemon rind
1 tsp lemon juice
1 tbs tamari
1 cup wholemeal bread crumbs
1 tsp crushed garlic
1 tsp coriander
1 tsp barley miso dissolved in water

Steam vegetables lightly. Mash tofu and add the rest of the ingredients and mix well. Form into patties and place on a greased tray and bake in the oven, turning once till brown (30 minutes). This mix can be placed in a greased loaf pan and baked in a moderate oven till browned. (In this recipe any cooked grain or legume can be used in place of tofu or tempeh.)

Salads

Almond rice salad (serves 2–3)

1½ cups brown rice
½ bunch spring onions (chopped)
1 cup chopped almonds
1 small red capsicum
1 tsp chopped garlic
tamari (to taste)

Cook and drain brown rice. Add other ingredients and gently mix together.

Baby lima bean salad (serves 2–3)

⅔ cup dried baby lima beans
¾ cup water
¼ tsp dried thyme
¼ tsp dried sage
½ cup finely diced fresh tomatoes
1 tsp freshly chopped parsley
2 bay leaves
½ cup diced celery
¼ tsp freshly chopped garlic

Preparation: 15 min
Cook: 40 min

Sort the lima beans, rinse and then soak overnight in water. Drain off soaking water, discard. Cook the beans for 30–40 minutes in 3 cups water with the bay leaves, thyme and sage. Cook until the beans are tender but are not falling apart. Remove the bay leaves and drain.

Toss the beans with the tomatoes, celery, parsley and garlic. Serve on a bed of mixed greens.

Bean and olive salad (serves 2–3)

$^2/_3$ cup dried beans of choice
$^1/_2$ cup each chopped celery and tomatoes
6 black olives chopped
1 dsp chopped chives
1 dsp chopped fresh mint

Preparation: 20 min
Cook: 40 min

Soak beans overnight in cold water. Discard soaking water from beans. Add fresh water to cover well and cook till tender. When done drain well and add other ingredients. Serve with French dressing.

Capsicum salad (serves 4)

1 red, 1 green, 1 yellow capsicum
200 g snow peas
$^1/_2$ tsp herbamare
1 tbs lemon juice
2 tsp tamari
1 tsp honey

Quarter capsicums, remove seeds and membranes. Slice into thin strips. Slice snow peas into thin strips. Put all dressing ingredients in jar and shake well.

Pour over vegetables. Serve with a cooked green.

Carrot salad (serves 2–3)

4 cups grated carrot
1 tbs chopped mint leaves
$^1/_2$ cup roughly chopped almonds
$^1/_2$ cup shredded coconut
$^1/_2$ cup yoghurt mixed with $^1/_4$ cup French dressing

Mix all together gently.

Corn salad with lemon dressing (serves 2–3)

1 cup fresh corn kernels (from 2 cobs)
$^1/_2$ tsp freshly chopped garlic
$^1/_2$ cup water
$^1/_2$ cup finely diced red capsicum
$^1/_2$ cup finely diced green capsicum
2 tbs chopped fresh coriander
1 tbs freshly chopped parsley
$^1/_8$ tsp cayenne
$^1/_2$ tsp herbamare
$^1/_4$ cup finely diced red onion

Dressing

1 tbs apple cider vinegar
2 tsp lemon juice
$^1/_2$ tsp honey
3 tbs fresh coriander (chopped)

Preparation: 30 min

Braise the corn with the garlic in the water for about 5 minutes. When the corn is cooked, toss with the diced capsicums, onion and seasonings. Mix the dressing and toss with the vegetables. Serve at room temperature.

Curried pasta salad (serves 2)

1 cup brown rice or 2 cups of pasta of choice
6 sliced radishes
½ bunch finely chopped spring onions
½ cup soy mayonnaise, thinned with
¼ cup soy milk
Curry powder as desired
2 chopped tomatoes
1 tsp chopped garlic

Cook pasta or rice, rinse and cool. Add other ingredients, fold gently through.

Dill and cucumber salad (serves 2)

4 sticks celery chopped
⅓ cup almonds
1 cucumber chopped

Place above ingredients in bowl. Mix with dressing which has been combined either by Bamix or food processing.

Dressing

1 cup soy yoghurt
1 tsp dill seeds, crushed
1 tsp lemon juice
2 tbs soy mayonnaise

Lentil salad (serves 2–3)

1½ cups dry lentils
6 cups water
½ cup finely diced onions
½ cup finely diced carrots
2 tbs chopped parsley
½ cup finely diced celery
½ cup finely diced tomatoes
3 bay leaves
1 tsp freshly chopped garlic
1 tbs chopped fresh thyme or 1 dsp dried thyme

Rinse lentils, then cook for 25–30 minutes in the 6 cups of water with the bay leaves until done. Do not overcook, or the lentils may fall apart. When the lentils are done, drain and toss them with the vegetables, parsley or other fresh herbs.

Green bean, beetroot salad with yoghurt dressing (serves 2)

1 cup chopped green beans
1 cup corn cut off the cob
1 medium beetroot grated
1 large spring onion chopped

Preparation: 30 min
Cook: 10 min

Steam beans and corn kernels until just

soft. Rinse in cold water, drain. In a bowl, mix beans, corn, onion and beetroot.

Dressing

2 tbs soy yoghurt
$\frac{1}{2}$ tsp crushed garlic
$\frac{1}{2}$ tsp cumin seeds

Whisk together dressing ingredients and pour over vegetables carefully and serve.

Italian pasta salad (serves 2–3)

175 g pasta of choice
1 cup sliced mushrooms
2 cups chopped tomatoes
$\frac{1}{2}$ cup sliced black olives
$\frac{1}{2}$ cup chopped green capsicum

Dressing

2 chopped spring onions
$\frac{1}{2}$ cup chopped parsley
1 tbs lemon juice
1 tsp Dijon mustard
1 tsp honey
2–3 tbs soy mayonnaise

Preparation: 30 min
Cook: 10 min

Cook pasta, drain and cool. Blend dressing ingredients. Mix all ingredients gently together.

Mung bean salad (serves 2)

2 cups fresh button mushrooms, thinly sliced
2 cups fresh mung bean sprouts, blanched and chilled
1 cup grated carrot
$\frac{1}{4}$ cup tamari
$\frac{1}{4}$ cup water

Blanch mung bean sprouts by covering with boiling water for 30 seconds, drain and refresh under cold water. Marinate mushrooms in tamari and water for half an hour, drain and add to carrot and sprouts.

Mung and millet salad (serves 2)

$\frac{3}{4}$ cups hulled millet
$\frac{1}{2}$ cup sliced green beans
$\frac{1}{2}$ cup mung bean sprouts
$\frac{1}{4}$ cup chopped spring onions
1 tbs tamari

Preparation: 10 min
Cook: 30 min

Cook millet and cool if salad is required cold. Lightly steam green beans and sprouts. Mix all ingredients. Can be served hot or cold.

Pasta and mushroom salad (serves 3–4)

200 g cooked pasta shells
2 cups sliced mushrooms
1 medium chopped onion
1 medium chopped capsicum
½ cup soy mayonnaise
½ cup chopped parsley
½ cup French type dressing

Mix dressing together and stir through pasta and vegetables.

Spinach salad (serves 2)

1 bunch spinach, shredded
6 black olives, sliced
6 cherry tomatoes, halved
½ cucumber, sliced
3 tbs almonds, sliced, toasted

Mix well and serve with garlic dressing.

Warm beetroot salad (serves 2)

2 large diced and cooked beetroot
1 tsp finely chopped spring onion
1 tbs finely chopped onion
½ cup chopped cucumber

Dressing

1 tsp chopped garlic
1 tsp dill seed
2 tbs cider vinegar
1 tsp honey

Mix dressing ingredients together and let stand for 1 hour if possible. Pour dressing over warm beetroot, onion and cucumber. Mix gently and serve.

Watercress salad (serves 2–3)

½ cup watercress sprigs
3 cups shredded cabbage
½ cup chopped parsley
½ cup alfalfa sprouts
1 cup diced tomato
⅔ cup French dressing

Wash watercress well and remove any tough stalks leaving watercress in sprigs. Add rest of ingredients. Stir dressing through. Serve with grain patties.

White bean salad (serves 2)

1 cup dried white beans
8 cups water
¼ cup finely diced carrots
⅓ cup diced tomato
¼ cup finely diced celery
1 cup freshly chopped parsley
1 tbs dried sage
5 bay leaves
lettuce

Sort and rinse the beans, then soak overnight in water. Drain the beans and put 8 cups water in a pot with the beans, bay leaves, and sage. Cook the beans for about 40 minutes, until tender. While the beans are cooking, combine the ingredients for the dressing. When the beans are cooked, remove the bay leaves and drain off the water. Toss the diced raw vegetables and dressing with the beans. Garnish with some extra chopped parsley, if desired, and serve on a bed of varied lettuces.

Dressing

1 tbs Dijon mustard
2½ tbs lemon juice
1½ tsp freshly minced garlic

Desserts

Apple crumble (serves 2–3)

6 apples sliced
½ cup roasted almonds chopped
1 cup rolled oats
½ cup currants
2 tsp lemon rind
2 tbs honey
2 tsp grated ginger
½ cup hot water

Put apples in greased baking dish and spread out evenly. Cover, then bake until soft. Put currants, ginger and lemon rind over apples. Separately dry roast almonds and oats, process half until finely chopped. Add to remaining oats. Mix in honey and water. Spread this topping evenly over apple mixture, cover and cook in preheated oven for about 20 mins at 200°. Remove cover and bake a further 5–10 mins until top is brown.

Apple strudel (serves 3–4)

3 sheets wholemeal filo pastry (if availabe, if not use usual filo)
2 tbs water
1 tbs apple juice
3 tbs raisins
½ cup bread crumbs
2 tbs honey
2½ cups thinly sliced apples
¼ tsp ground cinnamon
1 tbs vanilla extract

Keep pastry covered until ready to use. Mix honey and water and set aside. Peel, core and slice apples. Saute apples and apple juice, raisins, cinnamon and vanilla until they begin to soften. Add bread crumbs. Remove from heat and cool. Preheat oven to 175°. When cool assemble the filo pastry by laying filo down with short end of rectangle in front of you. Brush liberally with honey and water. Lay the next sheet down directly on top of first sheet and brush as before. Repeat with remaining layer. Spread the apple mixture evenly in the centre of the filo. Leave 4 cm border around filo rectangle. Starting at the short end, roll up filo in a roll. Put on greased tray. Twist ends to prevent mixture seeping out. Brush top with egg white. Bake approximately 30 minutes until golden brown. Let cool before cutting.

Apricot and peach crumble
(serves 3–4)

2 cups apricots, pitted and sliced
3 tbs wholemeal flour
1 cup partially ground muesli
5 cups pitted, sliced and peeled peaches
2 tsp arrowroot powder
½ cup honey
1 tsp cinnamon
1 tsp lemon juice

Preheat oven to 180°. Put the sliced fruit and lemon juice in bowl. Add honey. Stir the dry ingredients together then toss in with fruit. Put muesli into processor to break up a bit. Place fruit mixture in greased glass baking dish and top with muesli and bake for 40 minutes.

Baked apple with dried fruit filling

6 Granny Smith apples
2 cups mixed dried fruit
(sultanas, raisins, currants, apricots, and dates)
½ tsp nutmeg and
1 tsp cinnamon mixed

Combine fruit and spice. Core apples. Score around centre of apple by piercing skin with vegetable knife. This helps to retain the shape of the apple as it cooks. Fill core space with fruit mix. Press fruit firmly into cavity. Place in small baking dish with 2 cm water in bottom and a little honey drizzled over top. Cook 1 hour on 160°. Serve with yoghurt.

Baked bananas

3 large bananas
2 tbs water
yoghurt
½ cup honey
2 tbs lime or lemon juice

Preheat oven to 200°. Peel the bananas and cut them in half lengthwise. Place in flat baking dish. Mix honey, water and juice. Pour over bananas, bake for 15 minutes, basting periodically. Let cool and serve with a dollop of yoghurt.

Blueberry or strawberry cheesecake

Crust
2 cups rolled oats
½ cup apple juice concentrate

Place oats and apple juice concentrate in a food processor and blend until mixture binds together. You may need a little more apple juice concentrate. Press 'dough' into base of a greased pie plate. Bake for 15 mins.

Filling
300 g tofu
¼ cup agar agar flakes
1½ cups soy milk
¼ tsp vanilla essence

½ tsp grated lemon rind
2 tbs honey
1½ cups blueberries or
halved strawberries

Place all ingredients except berries in a blender and process till creamy. Transfer to a saucepan and stir until boiling. Take off heat and cool a little before pouring into cooked pie crust. Place berries decoratively on top of pie and refrigerate till firm.

Carob dinner mints

Carob
Soy powder
coconut
honey
1 tsp peppermint essence

Make up a basic carob ball mix. Add peppermint essence and enough water to bind. Spread mix evenly, about ½ cm thick on a greased tray. When firm cover with melted carob buds. Cut into squares. (Melt carob buds in bowl over boiling water.)

Custard

500 ml soy milk
300 ml water
2 tbs honey
1 dsp vanilla essence
2 heaped tbs corn flour

Heat soy milk, water, honey and vanilla to near boiling point. Dissolve corn flour in extra 200 ml water and add to mixture, boil for 1 minute.

Glazed fruit tart

1½ cups rolled oats
2 tbs apple juice concentrate
1 cup apple juice
1½ cups halved strawberries
15 seedless grapes halved
1 tbs arrowroot
2 peaches sliced
1 kiwi fruit sliced

Preheat oven to 225°. Pulse chop oats in a food processor for 10 seconds and mix with apple juice concentrate until it holds together. Pat into 20 cm greased pie pan and bake 10–15 minutes until browned. Let cool before filling. Gradually add the arrowroot to ¼ cup juice. Stir as the arrowroot is added to stop lumps. Pour into a saucepan with the rest of the juice. Heat over medium heat stirring constantly. The liquid will become cloudy, then crystal like and then start to boil. Boil for 3 minutes when it should become thicker than honey. Then cool. Arrange fruit in a pattern over pie crust. Pour a thin layer of fruit juice glaze over it. Refrigerate for 30 minutes before serving.

Jane's steamed pudding

2 cups dried mixed fruit
2 cups homemade soft bread crumbs
6 very ripe bananas mashed well
or pureed in food processor

Mix together. Place in a pudding basin, cover with greased greaseproof paper and steam for $1\frac{1}{2}$–2 hours in a saucepan with boiling water $\frac{1}{3}$ way up the basin.

Jelly

2 cups apple juice
$\frac{1}{2}$ cup apple juice concentrate
1 tbs agar agar or kanten flakes

Heat all together until boiling. Simmer and stir until flakes are dissolved. Pour into moulds or serving dishes. Allow to set. Any juice will do. Can add chopped cooked fruits. Just remember 1 dsp flakes to 1 cup liquid.

Lemon semolina pudding

$2\frac{1}{4}$ cups water
$\frac{1}{4}$ cup fresh lemon juice
3 tbs apple juice concentrate
$\frac{1}{2}$ cup semolina
3 tbs honey
1 tbs lemon zest
Fresh mint leaves to garnish

Bring the water to a boil and gradually whisk in the semolina, stirring to prevent lumps from forming. Keep stirring. Let cook about 10 minutes. Turn off the heat. Whisk in the lemon juice, honey, juice concentrate and zest. Cool. Serve garnished with mint leaves.

Poached pears and carob sauce (serves 4)

4 large unmarked pears
2 cups water
$\frac{1}{2}$ tbs honey
cinnamon
chopped nuts

Wash pears and place in a greased casserole dish. Pour over mixed water and honey. Bake in a moderate oven till tender approximately 45 minutes. Pour over sauce and sprinkle with a little cinnamon and chopped nuts.

Carob sauce

1 cup carob buds
1 tsp honey
1 cup soy yoghurt

Place carob buds in a stainless steel bowl over a pot half full of boiling water. Stir around till melted and whisk in the honey and soy yoghurt till emulsified. Keep over the hot water stirring till smooth.

Rice pudding

1½ cups brown rice
1 cup soy milk
¼ cup apple juice concentrate
or 2 tbs honey
1 cup diced fruit of your choice
½ cup raisins
2 cinnamon sticks
½ tsp vanilla extract
ground cinnamon for garnish

Cook rice in water, drain, return to saucepan then cover with soy milk. Bring to boil. Reduce heat and add cinnamon sticks, vanilla and apple juice concentrate. Continue stirring to prevent sticking when mixture has thickened, stir in honey. Add raisins and fruit. Remove cinnamon sticks and pour the rice pudding into serving dish. Dust with cinnamon.

Soy compound icing for cakes

2 cups soy compound
1 tbs honey
2 tbs lemon juice

Enough cold water to mix to a spreadable consistency. Apply icing fairly quickly as it will start to set almost immediately.

Alternatives

2 cups soy compound and ½ cup carob powder, water.

or
2 cups soy compound and 1 mashed banana; water if needed.

Sweet and spicy pumpkin pie

Filling
250 ml oat milk or soy milk
250 g tofu
½ cup honey
1½ cups cooked pumpkin
2 eggs
2 tbs lemon juice
4 tsp lemon zest
2 tsp vanilla
½ tsp ground cloves
½ tsp nutmeg
2 tsp cinnamon
1 tsp ground ginger

Base
Lightly toast 1½ cups rolled oats. Pulse chop half the oats in food processor for 10 seconds until fine. Add both lots together with enough apple juice concentrate to hold the oats together. Then press into a 20 cm tin. Set oven at 190°.

Filling
Mix all ingredients together until smooth. Pour over base in prepared tin and bake for approximately 1 hour or until pie is set. Let cool before serving.

Tofu cream for desserts and cakes

1 cup tofu
1 dsp vanilla essence
1 tsp cinnamon
1 dsp maple syrup

Emulsify in food processor or with a Bamix.

Tofu rice pudding

1 cup soft cooked brown rice
1 cup soy milk
1 small packet tofu (375 g)
$1/4$ cup currants
$1/4$ cup bread crumbs
$1/4$ cup honey
$1/4$ tsp cinnamon
$1/4$ tsp sea salt

Preheat the oven to 170°. Combine the tofu, soy milk, honey, salt and cinnamon and blend until smooth. Combine tofu mixture with the rice and currants and mix well. Spoon the mixture into a greased casserole or pie dish and sprinkle with the bread crumbs. Bake at 170° for 30–35 minutes or until set. Serve hot or cold.

Prune mousse (serves 3–4)

$1^{1}/2$ cups prunes (stoned)
1 tbs kanten flakes (or agar agar)
4 tbs water
2 cups soy yoghurt, plain or vanilla
1 tsp lemon juice
$1/2$ cup chopped almonds

Cook prunes in a little water till soft, then puree in a food processor. Dissolve the kanten or agar agar in the 4 tablespoons of water by placing it in a stainless steel bowl and place the bowl over a saucepan of simmering water. Stir till dissolved. Mix all ingredients together and pour into serving dishes. Allow to set and garnish with chopped almonds before serving.

Cakes

Banana cake

1 tbs yoghurt
$1/2$ cup melted butter
$1^{1}/2$ cups brown rice flour or
50:50 wholemeal flour
4 bananas, ripe and mashed
2 tsp baking powder substitute
1 egg beaten
$1/2$ cup honey

Combine rice flour, baking powder substitute. Combine wet ingredients and mix together with dry ingredients. Pour into prepared 20 cm tin. Bake approximately 1 hour at 180°.

Banana and date wholemeal scones

2 cups wholemeal flour
1 small banana mashed
1 tsp finely grated lemon rind
$^3/_4$ cup soy milk
1 cup dates very finely chopped
3 tsp baking powder substitute
$^1/_4$ tsp mixed spice
$^1/_4$ tsp cinnamon
1 tsp lemon juice

Sift dry ingredients twice. Add dates and lemon rind and mix through. Combine banana, milk and lemon juice. Add this to the flour and date mixture. Mix together and knead lightly. Cut into desired shapes. Place on lightly greased baking tray and cook at 230–250° for 15–20 minutes. Eat while still warm.

Blueberry and banana muffins

2 cups wholemeal flour
2 egg whites
1 cup raisins or sultanas
1 very ripe banana mashed
1 cup soy milk
$^1/_4$ cup bran
$^1/_4$ cup honey
$^1/_4$ cup apple juice concentrate
1 cup blueberries
2 tbs salt skip or other baking powder substitute

Preheat oven to 180°. Grease 1$^1/_2$ muffin trays with unsalted butter. Mix the flour, salt skip and bran in a bowl. Stir in the sultanas or raisins. In a blender or another bowl, mix together the banana, apple juice concentrate, milk, honey and egg whites. Add this mixture to the dry ingredients. Stir well. Gently fold in the blueberries. Spoon into muffin trays and bake for 15–20 minutes until muffins are just cooked. Cool 5 minutes in trays and then turn out onto wire rack.

Brownies

1 tbs egg substitute mixed with 2 tbs water or 1 egg
$^1/_3$ cup cocoa or carob powder
1 tsp vanilla
1 cup wholemeal flour
$^1/_2$ cup honey
1 tsp cinnamon
$^1/_4$ cup soy mayonnaise
$^3/_4$ cup almonds lightly toasted and chopped

Beat egg substitute and vanilla. Add honey, soy mayonnaise, cocoa, flour and spices. Stir in nuts, put into greased square pan and bake 25 minutes at 170°.

Carrot ginger cake

1$^1/_2$ cups wholemeal flour
$^1/_2$ cup honey
$^3/_4$ cup soy milk
1 cup carrots finely grated
1 egg

½ cup raisins

2 tbs melted butter

¾ tsp cinnamon

3½ tsp salt skip or other baking pwder substitute

1 tsp grated fresh ginger

½ tsp freshly grated nutmeg

Preheat oven to 180°. Sift flour and cinnamon into a large bowl. Mix the egg, butter, soy milk, ginger and honey separately in a blender, fold or whisk them into the dry mixture (do not over mix). Stir in the carrots and raisins and spoon the batter into a prepared cake pan. Bake for 35 minutes at 170°. Let stand in pan for 15 minutes before inverting onto platter. Chill. Optional additions: 1 cup pineapple chunks, ¾ cup chopped walnuts.

Pikelets

2 cups wholemeal flour

1 tbs egg substitute or 1 egg

50:50 soy milk and water

1 tsp baking powder

1 tsp honey

Place flour and baking powder in a bowl, add egg, honey and enough soy milk to make thin mixture. Cook in spoonfuls in stainless steel crepe pan using butter to grease pan.

Polenta cake

4 cups water

⅓ cup honey

2 cups polenta

½ cup chopped almonds

⅓ cup maple syrup

¾ cup sultanas

3 tsp grated lemon rind

½ tsp ground cinnamon

Heat water, maple syrup and honey to near boiling, reduce heat. Gradually add polenta, stirring all the time. Cook for about 10 minutes. Remove from heat and stir in lemon rind, sultanas and almonds. Turn into a prepared (lightly greased) 20 cm springform pan. Sprinkle with cinnamon, cook in moderate oven for 15 minutes. Cool and remove from tin.

Spiced muffins

1 cup wholemeal flour

1 cup unbleached flour

1 cup soy milk

2 tbs apple juice concentrate

4 tsp salt skip or other baking powder substitute

1 tsp cinnamon

¼ tsp nutmeg

2 tbs apricot jam

Sift flours. Sift again with baking powder and spices, returning the bran to the bowl. Make a well. Combine the milk, apple juice concentrate and apricot jam thoroughly and pour all at once into the well. Using definite circular strokes, scraping the bottom and sides of the bowl, mix liquid into flour until just combined, about 12 strokes. The dough should be moist but lumpy. Spoon mixture into greased muffin pans, filling cups about two thirds full. Bake at 190° for 25 minutes.

Variations

Add ¾ cup chopped dates or natural sultanas to the dry ingredients before adding liquid.

Wheat free carob brownies

1 cup grated apple
½ cup chopped almonds
¾ cup carob powder
2 cups rolled oats soaked in ½ cup water for 10 minutes
1 tsp vanilla
½ cup melted unsalted butter

Combine all well in a bowl. Let stand for 15 minutes. Spoon into a lightly greased 25 cm pan and bake approximately 25 minutes at 200°. Cut when cool.

Children's recipes

Potato chips

Potatoes

Scrub required amount of potatoes. Cut into fat wedges. Place skin side down on a greased oven tray. Cover with another tray or greased greaseproof paper. Put in moderate oven. Let steam till nearly cooked. Remove cover and increase oven heat to allow wedges to crisp and brown. Sprinkle with herbamare if liked.

Vegetable burgers

4 cups grated vegetables of choice
1/4 cup chopped spring onion
1 tbs mixed herbs
1/2 cup chopped parsley
1 cup crumbled tofu
2 tbs tamari
1 cup wholemeal bread crumbs
1 clove crushed garlic
1 egg or 1/2 cup wholemeal flour
A little water if needed to hold mix together

Steam vegetables lightly. Mix all together in a bowl and divide into four. Shape each portion into a ball then flatten a little. Coat in crumbs, bran or rice bran. Place on a lightly greased tray or in an electric fry pan and cook approximately 30 minutes. Turning once. Oven temperature, moderate.

Vegetable sticks in pastry

Vegetables of choice
2 sheets filo pastry

Cut vegetables (i.e. carrots, sweet potato, parsnip or potato) into finger sized pieces. Steam till just tender. Cut two sheets of filo pastry into 7 or 8 cm squares. Lay a piece of vegetable on each square diagonally. Sprinkle with herbamare and roll up, leaving each end open to expose the tip of the vegetable. Place on a lightly greased oven tray and bake till golden. About 10–15 minutes in a moderate oven. Can brush with a little egg yolk and sprinkle with seeds of choice before cooking.

Easy dipping chips

Sorj or Mountain Bread

Cut sheets of the bread into shapes with scissors; square, diamond etc. For a different taste you can brush sheets with tamari before cutting. Spread out on a baking sheet and dry in the oven till crisp. Will keep in a sealed jar for several weeks.

Carob sauce

1 cup carob buds
1 tsp honey
1 cup soy yoghurt

Place carob buds in a stainless steel bowl over a pot half full of boiling water. Stir around till melted and whisk in the honey and soy yoghurt till emulsified. Keep over the hot water stirring till smooth.

Apple jelly

4 cups apple juice
3 dsp agar agar or Kanten flakes
$1/2$ cup apple juice concentrate

Heat all together. Simmer and stir until flakes are dissolved. Pour into moulds or serving dishes. Allow to set. Decorate with fresh fruit and mint leaves.

Banana dessert

250 g silken tofu
1 medium ripe banana
1 tbs vanilla
$1/2$ cup soy milk
3 dsp arrowroot

Place all ingredients in a saucepan and puree with a bamix. Place on heat and whisk gently till mixture boils. Simmer 3–4 minutes, still stirring gently. Pour into serving glasses or boats. Decorate with some fresh fruit slices or chopped nuts. Chill several hours before serving.

Chewy double carob chip cookies

$1/2$ cup dates, pitted
2 tsp vanilla extract
$1/2$ tbs baking powder
20 almonds (optional)
1 cup fruit juice (apple, berry etc)
$1/2$ cup wholemeal flour
$1/2$ cup carob chips
$1/2$ cup each oatbran and wheat bran

Preheat oven to 350°. Pulse chop the dates and the fruit juice in a food processor. Add vanilla and puree several seconds. Stir together the bran, flour and baking powder, then pulse chop them in the processor with the juice mixture. Transfer to a medium bowl. Stir in the carob chips and roll the cookie dough into 1" balls. Press down the almond in the centre, if desired. Bake at 350° for 12 to 15 minutes. Store in airtight bag, otherwise these soft, chewy cookies get hard after 2–3 days because they are made without shortening.

Reflections

Deep Peace

Deep peace of the running wave to you,
Deep peace of the flowing air to you,
Deep peace of the quiet earth to you,
Deep peace of the shining stars to you,
Deep peace of the gentle night to you,
Moon and stars pour their healing light on you.

Deep peace of Christ—the Light of the world to you.
Adapted from an old Gaelic rime,

John Rutter

Old Folks Are Worth a Fortune

Old folks are worth a fortune. Silver in their hair,
gold in their teeth, stones in their kidneys,
and gas in their stomachs.
I have become a little older since I saw you last
and a few things have changed in my life.

Frankly I have become a frivolous old girl,
I'm seeing five gentlemen every day.

As soon as I wake, Will Power helps me out of bed.
Then I go to my Lou. Next it's time too for Uncle Toby
to come along, and then it's time for Billy Tea.
They leave and Arthur Itis shows up and stays with me
for the rest of the day. He doesn't like to stay in one
place so he takes me from joint to joint.

After such a long day, I'm really tired and glad to

go to bed with Johnny Walker. What a life.
Oh yes, I'm also flirting with Al Zymer.
P.S.
The preacher came to call the other day.
He said that at my age I should be thinking
about the hereafter. Oh I said, I do all the time.
No matter where I am, if I'm in the kitchen or out
in the garden I ask myself, 'Now what am I here after.'

To Dorothy

We drove through the dust at the gate. We limped down the drive,
with bleeding hearts and bleeding brains. Dust and guts laid bare to the crows.
The days passed.
Trevor rocked me in his peace, Bob's voice soothed me, and soothed me again
when I was frightened.
But Dorothy beat me into submission.
The flicks and the pictures ripped into me.
The walks and talks dribbled out and ran down the hill to the river.
I cried and slept and was tired a lot. I crossed my arms against the world.
But Dorothy, in a quiet way, terrified me.

I could hear the worry and fear, I could see the doubt and coughs and pain.
I feel beneath the noise and was frightened by the silence.
I looked for a chapel and couldn't find one but I found the dandelion meadow and
    the kangaroo who watched me.
We'll get well, for Dorothy.

Kate Beattie

Meditation at Yarra Valley

Down past Yarra Junction
In the meeting hall
Bob takes meditation
Whilst we sit round the walls
And while we all have our eyes shut tight

142

Willie spends his time looking for the light
I'm worried about my drawing
I didn't see what they could see
Gosh who is that snoring?
I'm glad that it's not me.

Meanwhile in the kitchen
without a lot of fuss
Dorothy prepares a meal
to give to all of us.
And although we've all been told to chew a lot
You can tell by the sounds in here that some of us forgot
This place is so relaxing
I really like Tai Chi
But I still don't know why Tibor
touches Ross instead of me.

Because of meditation
We have most restful nights
But Trevor seems to wake us up
as soon as it gets light.
So while we're doing stretching and meditating as well
Most of us make plans as to where to stick that bell.

I'm still worried about my drawing
It seems very Freudian to me
I can still hear that snoring
I hope it isn't me.

Bruce Graham

The Gawler Waltz

We have travelled far and wide
Us Aussies and our Kiwi friends
To Ian's place in the sunshine state Victoria
We've sat and we've talked and waited till the ding-a-ling

Let's give thanks for it's time for a pee.

Chorus:

Meditate and eat our greens
Meditate and eat our greens
Un-til we end up just a little loose!
And the rumbles can be heard
From each and every one of us
Thanks to Dorothy and her dietaries!

Here we are together right out in the Aussie bush
Under the gumtrees with the kangaroos
And we rant and we crave for some chocolate, beer and take-a-way
But we've got a goal that we're gonna stick too.

Chorus:

Dorothy our speaker adds her daily comments
'You'll never catch me "sleeping in"' says she
And we sing and we dance like Indians who are in a trance
You won't get a-rest when you come to stay here.

Chorus:

Now it is time for us to say good bye to all
Thank you to Ian, Nan and Sue
Thank you staff and thank you all our group too
We'll come a waltzing Gawler style with you!
We'll come a waltzing Gawler style with you!

Job to Do

This is a story about four people
named Everybody, Somebody, Anybody and Nobody.
There was an important job to be done and Everybody was asked to do it.
Everybody was sure that Somebody would do it.
Anybody could have done it, But Nobody did it.
Somebody got angry about that because it was Everybody's job.

Everybody thought Anybody could do it,
but Nobody realised that Everybody woudn't do it.
It ended up that Everybody blamed Somebody when actually Nobody asked
   Anybody.

Attitude

Our deepest fear is not that we are inadequate;
Our deepest fear is that we are powerful beyond measure.
It is our light, not our darkness that most frightened us.
We ask ourselves, who am I to be brilliant, gorgeous, talented and fabulous?

Actually who are you not to be?
You are a child of God.
Your playing small doesn't serve the world.
There is nothing enlightened about shrinking so that other people won't feel
   insecure around you.
We were born to magnify the glory of God that is within us.
It's not just in some of us, it's in everyone.

And as we let our own light shine, we unconsciously give other people permission
   to do the same.
As we are liberated from our own fear, our presence automatically liberates others.

From Nelson Mandela's speech.
Poem written by Marianne Williamson.

Today ... Joy

There are two days in every week about which we should not worry,
   two days which should be kept from fear and apprehension.

One of these days is Yesterday with its mistakes and cares, its faults and blunders,
its aches and pains.
Yesterday has passed forever beyond our control.

All the money in the world cannot bring back Yesterday. We cannot erase a
single word we said. Yesterday is gone.

The other day we should not worry about is Tomorrow with its possible adversities, its burdens, its large promise, and poor performance.

Tomorrow is also beyond our immediate control.

Tomorrow's sun will rise, either in splendour or behind a mask of clouds—but it will rise.

Until it does, we have no stake in Tomorrow, for it is yet unborn.

This leaves only one day—today. Any person can fight the battles of just one day.

It is only when you and I add the burdens of those two awful eternities—Yesterday and Tomorrow—that we break down.

It is not the experience of today that drives us mad—it is remorse or bitterness for somethng which happened Yesterday and the dread of what will happen Tomorrow.

If you do your best every day Yesterday will not matter—and Tomorrow should hold no fear.

Something I Would Like to Thank the Group for

Ian Gawler is our inspiration,
First we learned our meditation
From him and Bob, his right hand man
Well supported by the Duchess, Nan.
Dorothy and her staff have fed us well
A fart—or burp—what the hell,
Peter in garden toils
He has made us mindful of the soils.
Tai Chi with Tibor—O dear Joan
Will you ever do Yoga without a moan?
If I were a poet laureate,
I'd write a verbal minute
For everyone.
But that must wait until the time
When Felix brings for us the wine.

Our work together has been a test
Which challenged everything within our chest
Tears have flowed and are a sign
That your healing has begun—as has mine
In our juices we rejoice
And even with the green—we have a choice
To the group I say a special thanks
Our friends, no doubt will think we're cranks
And to the group I give my love
A bond so strong I take with me
To help me heal and I hope thee
Tomorrow, we must part
And sadly we will leave, but with an open heart.

Jill Need

The Invitation

It doesn't interest me what you do for a living.
I want to know what you ache for.
I dare to dream of meeting your heart's longing.
It doesn't interest me how old you are.
I want to know if you will risk looking like a fool for love,
For your dreams,
For the adventure of being alive.
It doesn't interest me what planets are squaring your moon
I want to know if you have touched the centre of your own sorrow,
If you have been opened by life's betrayals,
Or have become shrivelled and closed from fear of future pain!
I want to know if you can sit with pain, mine or your own,
Without moving to hide it or fade it or fix it.
I want to know if you can be with joy.
Mine or your own;
If you can dance with wildness
And let ecstasy fill you to the tips of your fingers and toes
Without cautioning us to be careful,
Or to remember the limitations of being human.

It doesn't interest me if the story you are telling me is true
I want to know if you can disappoint another
To be true to yourself;
If you can bear the accusation of betrayal and not betray your own soul.
I want to know if you can see beauty even when it's not pretty every day.
And if you can source your life from its presence.
I want to know if you can live with failure, yours or mine, and still stand on the
    edge of a lake and shout to the silver moon, 'YES!'
It doesn't interest me to know where you live,
Or how much money you have
I want to know if you can get up after the night of grief and despair,
Weary and bruised to the bone
And do what needs to be done for the children.
It doesn't interest me who you are,
Or how you came to be here.
I want to know if you will stand in the centre of the fire with me, and not shrink
    back.
It doesn't interest me where or what or with whom you have studied.
I want to know what sustains you from the inside when all else falls away.
I want to know if you can be alone with yourself,
And if you truly like the company you keep in the empty moments.

Native American Elder

If It Is Not Too Dark

Go for a walk if it is not too dark.
Get some fresh air, try to smile.
Say something kind
To a safe-looking stranger, if one happens by.
Always exercise your heart's knowing.
You might as well attempt something real
Along this path.
Take your spouse or lover into your arms
The way you did when you first met.
Let tenderness pour from your eyes
The way the Sun gazes warmly on the earth.

Play a game with some children.
Extend yourself to a friend.
Sing a few ribald songs to your pets and plants—
Why not let them get drunk and wild?
Let's toast
Every rung we've climbed on evolution's ladder.
Whisper, 'I love you! I love you!'
To the whole mad world.
Let's stop reading about God—
We will never understand him.
Jump to your feet, wave your fists,
Threaten and warn the whole universe
That your heart can no longer live
Without real love!

I Am

I am life.
I am spirit.
I am consciousness.
I am worthy and valuable.
I am nature's greatest miracle.
I am a unique and precious human being.

No one in the universe is quite the same or has exactly the same impact on the world as my own unique and precious self.

Even though my awareness may differ, from others, my worthiness is absolutely equal with all, for no one in the world is more or less important than I am.

My loyalty is firstly to my true self and what's true for me. I have no need to worship others' opinions. I stand up for my own values.

I am my own authority. I think for myself and act accordingly.

I am in charge of my own thoughts and images. This way I am consciously in charge of my own life. I can create for myself as I choose. I have inner strength, wisdom and compassion, sufficient enough to handle everything I will encounter.

Knowing I am not my actions, I allow myself the freedom to make mistakes and to be defeated without feeling guilty or inferior.

I give myself the freedom to be wrong, to fail, and to be less than perfect. I defer to no one on account of their wealth, power or prestige, I can say no.

Even when I know it will displease others. I do not let others talk me into things against my better judgement. I do not deny my own needs, feelings or what's true for me in order to please others. I acknowledge I am without blame or guilt, for in the whole of my life, in every situation, I know I have always done the best I could, with what I knew and the circumstances I was in at the time, and I always will. In giving up all reasons for remorse or guilt or blame or shame to do with any past actions, I now have warm and loving feelings towards myself, for I am totally worthy and have every reason to have a high opinion of myself.

I refrain from all value judging or having expectations of others, and I am free of resentment and bitterness. I allow all people the right to their own unique awareness.

I do not allow personal comparisons to effect my sense of worth. I do not try to prove my worth by accomplishments. I realise I cannot prove or disprove my worth by what I do.

My very existence proves my innate worth and importance.

I am patient, kind and gentle with myself.

I am OK all right.

My number one responsibility is my own life and well-being. I therefore have the innate authority and freedom to satisfy my own needs first.

I acknowledge that everything I recognise as good and beautiful in another must also be in me to enable me to recognise it in the other. I live and cherish my wonderful, precious self, for I accept myself totally and unconditionally.

As the soul, I am an indestructible spiritual being.

I AM ENOUGH

By a Young Teenage Girl

Grace

Thank you, O Lord and Lady God, that we may eat from your bountiful table.

You feed us, you nourish us at all times with your word, your spirit and our food, physical and pure.

God, good and loving, feed thus all your children on Earth and leave no child to starve or thirst, but create, through your son, a world abundant to all living here.

Forgiveness Affirmations

I fully and freely forgive (name) for all his/her actions, past, present and future and I release him/her to his/her highest good.

(Say 15 times per day at least, for months and months)

The Peace Candle

Several years ago in London, a young man named Chris was diagnosed with leukaemia. His doctor informed him that his death was imminent and he could not expect to live longer than 3–6 months. He was advised to go home and make his arrangements. Chris went home and completely fell apart for three weeks. When all his anger was spent and he had no more tears left to cry, he began to feel urgency about making the very best use of the little time he had left. He thought about what the world needed most and decided, as most people would, that it had to be 'world peace'. So he resolved to set about devoting himself whole-heartedly to this end.

Possessions no longer were a priority in Chris's life seeing as he would not be needing them after a couple of months, so he sold what he had and used the money to print leaflets aimed at raising people's awareness of the need for world peace. These he handed out to anyone who would take them on street corners all over London.

As the medical profession were unable to offer Chris any hope of recovery, he decided to take the matter into his own hands and at least aim for the highest possible quality of whatever life he had left. He saw an advertisement for Reiki and was attuned to levels one and two. This introduced him to an awareness of his spirituality which he keenly pursued.

Three months passed, six months passed, and he was still handing out leaflets. Unfortunately though, his money was fast running out, so he used the last of his funds to start a small business for himself making candles and painting T-shirts with a world peace logo on them. He sold these on street corners to finance the printing of leaflets and to pay for his rent and food.

One year passed, two years passed, three years passed and Chris was still handing out leaflets and selling candles and T-shirts. He was at a social event one evening when he met the doctor who had diagnosed his illness three years earlier. The doctor was astounded to see Chris not only alive, but apparently quite well. He convinced Chris to admit himself into hospital for tests. Everyone was amazed to find that all traces of leukaemia had disappeared.

Time passed, and once when the Dalai Lama was visiting London on a lecture tour, Chris went along to hear him speak. Afterwards he went backstage and told his story to the Dalai Lama's helpers. He requested an audience with the Dalai Lama the following day. The helpers agreed, and Chris arrived at the appointment with one of his handmade candles. He asked the Dalai Lama to light his candle and dedicate it to world peace with the idea that all candles lit from that one would carry with it his blessing and dedication.

At midnight on 1 January 1997, thousands of candles had been known to be lit from the original and some were taken to at least five different countries. If this story and the flame is shared by all those who come in contact with it, by January 2000, millions of peple all over the world will be lighting candles and directing their thoughts and energies to the concept of world peace.

Imagine if you will, the awesome power generated by such an act and the potential positive impact this could have on humankind. Perhaps you have said to yourself 'I am only one person, how can my meagre efforts possibly make a difference to the scheme of things?' Here is your answer—positive changes on a global level need only require a small effort by individuals and this is your chance to participate. Enjoy!

Love and Light

Healing Affirmations

(Affirmations are healing words which sink deep into the subconscious)

An infinite flow of success and abundance, prosperity, health and happiness is mine ... NOW!

I have faith in the healing power of the universe as it works mightily in me ... NOW!

I have faith that all things are working together for my good ... NOW!

I have faith in the perfect outcome of every situation in my life because the universe is in absolute control, and my faith keeps me whole.

I am a tower of strength within and without ... NOW!

I let all burdens fall from my shoulders and all anxieties from my mind ... NOW!

I let all fears slip away from my heart and I let every shackle be loosened ... NOW!

Divine strength is making wise and true adjustments in every phase of my life ... NOW!

I now forgive all apparent injustices. I forgive myself for first having set them in motion.

Divine justice now moulds my present and my future perfectly.

Love transforms, love transfigures, love fills my heart with harmony, love fills my life to overflowing with happiness and peace ... NOW!

I am shown what to do in all circumstance and in all places ... NOW!

I am aware of what I need to know. When I need to know it. I express wisdom and understanding and make the right decisions quickly ... NOW!

My mind is guided now by divine intelligence. I unleash my spiritual forces now. I am unfettered and unbound. I am free with freedom of spirit.

I willingly let go of every thought, condition or relationship which in any way retards my perfect healing ... NOW!

I am blessed with perfect elimination in my mind, body and relationships ... NOW!

I willingly release the thoughts and things which clutter my life. For I forgive myself and others ... NOW!

Nan Lasry

Attitude

The longer I live, the more I realise the impact of attitude on life.

Attitude, to me is more important than the past, than education, than money, than success, than what other people think or say or do.

It is more important than appearance, giftedness or skill.

It will make or break a company ... a church ... a home.

The remarkable thing is you have a choice every day regarding the attitude you will embrace for that day.

We cannot change the inevitable ... the only thing we can do is play on the one string we have, and that is our attitude.

I am convinced that life is 10 per cent what happens to me and 90 per cent how I react to it.

And so it is with you ... you are in charge of your attitude.

Author Unknown

Perform Random Acts of Kindness and Senseless Beauty

It's a crisp winter day in San Francisco. A woman in a red Honda drives up to the Bay Bridge tollbooth. 'I'm paying for myself and six cars behind me', she says with a smile, handing over seven commuter tickets. One after another, the next six drivers arrive at the tollbooth, dollars in hand, only to be told, 'Some lady up ahead paid your fare. Have a nice day!'

The woman in the Honda, it turns out, had read something on an index card taped to a friend's refrigerator. Perform Random Acts of Kindness and Senseless Beauty.' The phrase seemed to leap out at her, and she copied it down.

Judy Foreman spotted the same phrase spray-painted on a warehouse wall a hundred miles from her home. It stayed on her mind for days, so she gave up and drove all the way back to copy it down. 'I thought it was incredibly beautiful,' she said, explaining why she's taken to writing it at the bottom of all of her letters. 'It's like a message from above.'

Her husband, Frank, liked the phrase so much that he put it up on the wall for his seventh-graders, one of whom was the daughter of a local columnist. The columnist put it in the paper, admitting that though she liked it, she didn't know where it came from or what it really meant.

Two days later the columnist heard from Anne Herbert. Tall, blonde and forty, Anne lives in Marin, one of the country's richest counties, where she house-sits, takes odd jobs and gets by. It was in a Sausalito restaurant that Ms Herbert jotted the phrase down on a paper place mat after turning it around in her mind for days. 'That's wonderful,' a man sitting nearby said and copied it down carefully on his own place mat.

Says Ms Herbert, 'Kindness can build upon itself as much as violence can.' Now the phrase is spreading, on bumper stickers, on walls, at the bottom of letters and business cards. And as it spreads, so does a vision of guerilla goodness.

In Portland, Oregon, a man plunks a coin into a stranger's meter just in time. In Paterson, New Jersey, a dozen people with pails and mops and tulip bulbs descend on a run-down house and clean it from top to bottom while the owners look on, dazed and smiling. In Chicago, a teenage boy is shovelling off his driveway when an impulse strikes what the hell, nobody's looking, he thinks and shovels the neighbour's driveway too.

It's positive anarchy, disorder, a sweet disturbance. A woman in Boston writes Merry Christmas to the teller on the back of her cheques. A man in St Louis, whose car has just been rear-ended by a young woman waves her away saying, 'It's just a scratch, don't worry'.

Senseless acts of beauty spread. A man plants daffodils along the roadway, his shirt billowing in the breeze from passing cars. In Seattle, a man appoints himself a one-man vigilante sanitation servant and roams the concrete jungle collecting litter in a supermarket cart. In Atlanta, a man scrubs graffiti from a park bench.

They say you can't smile without cheering yourself up a little. Likewise, you can't commit an act of random kindness without feeling as if your own troubles have been lightened, if only because the world has become a slightly better place. And you can't be a recipient without feeling a shock, a pleasant jolt. If you were one of those rush hour drivers who found your bridge toll paid, who knows what you might have been inspired to do for someone else later on: wave someone on in the intersection? Smile at a tired clerk? Or something larger, greater?

Like all revolutions, guerilla goodness begins slowly, with a single act. Let it be yours!

This summer my wife and I were resting a few hours in a wonderful spiritual bookstore in Santa Fe. In walked a being that could have easily passed for Pan. He picked up a bamboo flute and started to pay an exquisite tune. His eyes were closed, and he and flute looked like they had been old friends from ancient times. When he finished playing he quietly held the flute in his lap. 'Why don't you take it home with you?' we asked. 'Haven't got the money,' said he. 'I just wanted to stop in to see if it was still here.'

Quietly, we got up and went to the register and purchased it for him. With the receipt in hand, we returned to him. 'It's yours now,' we told him. His eyes grew wide with delight and disbelief. 'I must tell you something,' he said. 'I hate bumper stickers usually but as I was walking into this bookstore there was a car in the parking lot that had a bumper sticker with one of the most beautiful phrases I ever heard. When I sat down to play this flute, it was that very phrase that inspired the piece you heard me play.'

I don't think I need to tell you what bumper sticker he saw!

As these stories reveal, displaying this bumper sticker can have the most wonderful results!

God Will Supply

When skies have turned dark
And there seems not a spark
If hope is at hand
For the day;
When adverse winds blow,
What a comfort to know
That God supplies

Light for the way!
When in deep despair
And surrounded by care,
And you sink 'neath
The weight of the load,
What a joy and what peace,
And what blessed release
When God supplies
Strength for the road!
So lift up your eyes
And your faith to the skies,
Being certain there's
Someone who heeds
Each murmured request
In the way that is best,
For God will supply
All your needs!

Jon Gilbert

Morning Bells

Morning bells, morning bells, Trevor's on the prowl
Just as soon as we wake up
Our stomachs start to growl

Hey!

Rumbling bowels, rumbling bowels,
Rumble all the way
When somebody wants to go, don't stand in their way!

Hey

Dashing to the loo, waiting in the queue
Wondering if we'll ever be, able to do a —

Hey

Crying eyes, laughing eyes, sharing in all ways
What a joy it is to be in loving company

Hey

Visualise, affirmise, meditate all day
Once we've got the hang of this
They'll let us get away.

Hey!

The Healing Journey

We move forward without fear
But let them hear
We hurt inside
Our emotions flow like a tide
Are you on our side
Or will you move aside.

Moving forward involves pain
But with so much to gain
The risks may be high
But the need to try is sounded in a cry
A cry from within
A cry lost in the noise
A cry found again
In the silence behind the noise.

Nicole Edyvane

Trevor's Affirmation Song

Farewell to my cancer forever
Goodbye to all tumours and lumps

Farewell to those nasty free radicals
My immune system's coming up trumps

Singing too roo it's all in my attitude
I'm 100 per cent all the way
I'm giving this illness no latitude . . .
Getting better and better each day

So to all of you doctors and specialists
Who tell me how I should behave
I am sure that I'm going to surprise you
One day I will dance on your grave!

Instructions For Life

1 Take into account that great love and great achievements involve great risk.
2 When you lose, don't lose the lesson.
3 Follow the three R's: Respect for self, Respect for others and Responsibility for all your actions.
4 Remember that not getting what you want is sometimes a wonderful stroke of luck.
5 Learn the rules so you know how to break them properly.
6 Don't let a little dispute injure a great friendship.
7 When you realise you've made a mistake, take immediate steps to correct it.
8 Spend some time alone every day.
9 Open your arms to change, but don't let go of your values.
10 Remember that silence is sometimes the best answer.
11 Live a good, honourable life. Then when you get old and think back, you'll be able to enjoy it a second time.
12 A loving atmosphere in your home is the foundation for your life.
13 In disagreements with loved ones, deal only with the current situation; don't bring up the past.
14 Share your knowledge. It's a way to achieve immortality.
15 Be gentle with the earth.
16 Once a year, go some place you've never been before.
17 Remember that the best relationship is one in which your love for each other exceeds your need for each other.

18 Judge your success by what you had to give up in order to get it.

19 Approach love and cooking with reckless abandon.

Pass this mantra on to at least five people and your life will improve:

0–4 people and your life will improve slightly,

5–9 people and your life will improve to your liking,

9–14 people and you will have at least five surprises in the next three weeks,

15 people and above and your life will improve drastically and everything you ever dreamed of will begin to take shape.

Dalai Lama

Cancer

I walked out from the doctor's
And I did it in a trance,
I had wasted half a lifetime
And used up my last chance.
I had used it up on dreaming
Of the way it should have been,
And life in all its beauty
I hadn't even seen.

They said I needed treatment
And I weighed up all the odds,
Like a little kid in first grade
'cept I didn't use the rods.
It was all so overwhelming
I walked in a sort of haze,
The fact that seemed to glare at me
Was 'my life is now in days'.

'Don't take it as a sentence
Rise above it,' they all said.
Not so easy when you face it
And your heart just feels like lead;
Now, I'm not one to grumble

And I can take it on the chin,
So, I decided quietly
I can fight this thing and win.

My friends, they gather round me
And fill me with new hope,
I've lots of things I want to do
No time to sit and mope;
I'll see my kids grown up
And safely on their way,
No need for me to leave just yet
So, I'll refuse and stay.

There's lots of things I've not tried
Will keep me on this earth,
It's time I put them to the test
And make them prove their worth;
I have this thing inside me
Faith, it's called, by some,
And a little voice that tells me
My time has not yet come.

Pauline Lindley

Waltzing with Ian

Once a jolly cancer patient went to the doctor
Off to the surgeon with you said he
So they cut and they stitched
As they searched for the tumour
You'll come a waltzing to theatre with me.
Waltzing to theatre ... Waltzing to theatre
You'll come a waltzing to theatre with me
And we'll snip and we'll cut and you'll wake up in recovery
You'll come a waltzing to theatre with me.

Up came the radiologist

Mounted on his linear accelerator
We're going to burn you alive said he
So they fried and they frazzled
As I lay there in agony
You'll come a waltzing to therapy with me.
Waltzing to therapy ... Waltzing to therapy
You'll come a waltzing to therapy with me
And I cried and I wept as they burnt the shit out of me
You'll come a waltzing to therapy with me.

Next came the chemo
With drugs one, two and three
You have a special mixture said he
And I chucked and spewed
While they told me it was good for me
You'll come a waltzing to chemo with me.
Waltzing to chemo ... Waltzing to chemo
You'll come a waltzing to chemo with me
And I chucked and spewed
While they told me it was good for me
You'll come a waltzing to chemo with me.

Up jumped the cancer patient
And ran to Yarra Valley
Ian, carrot juice and meditation for me
And the giggles and the laughter
May be heard around the centre
You'll come a waltzing with Ian and me.
Waltzing with Ian ... Waltzing with Ian
You'll come a waltzing with Ian and me
And the laughter may be heard as it echoes through the valley
You'll come a waltzing with Ian and me.

Mary O'Doherty

To Those Whom I Love, and Those Who Love Me

When I am gone, release me, let me go,
I have so many things to see and do.
You must not tie yourself to me with tears,
Be happy that we had so many years.
You can only guess how much you gave me,
In happiness.
I thank you for the love you each have shown,
And now it's time I travelled on alone.
So grieve a while for me, if grieve you must,
Then let your grief be comforted by trust.
It's only for a while that we must part,
So bless the memories within your heart
I will not be far away—for life goes on,
So if you need me call, and I will come.
Though you cannot see or touch me, I'll be near,
And if you listen with your heart, you will hear,
All of my love around you, soft and clear
Then, when you must come this way alone,
I will greet you with a smile, and a 'welcome home'.

Betty Goding

The Wild Rover—Reflections on the 7-day Program

On the last day of a 7-day program, Trevor delighted everyone with his rendition of 'The Wild Rover'—sung with a definite lilt! Here is the edited version:

I've been a wild rover for many a year
But I've never struck anythin' like I've struck 'ere . . .
At a Centre out 'ere midst the rolling green hills
They do nothin' but focus on all yer ills.

CHORUS:
An' it's no, no never

Never anywhere else
Never ever before 'ave I seen
A place so obsessed with yer 'ealth.

If a bloke wants a smoke or a wee 'armless drink
There's people out 'ere makes 'im first stop and think
Think of 'is lungs and think of 'is 'eart,
They say ya gotta stop now and make a fresh start.

They started the rot when—must like back in school
They made us draw pictures—I felt such a fool!
Their trick was to get me to let it all out
Then they'd somehow interpret what me life's all about.

We did breathin' and chantin' of every kind . . .
Relaxin' the body and stillin' the mind.
But 'tho I felt like a rag doll . . . me head was still buzzin'
With thoughts floodin' through at fourteen to the dozen.

Images and visions and bright healing lights
We did it ad nauseam from mornin' till night
It annoyed me to do it at Ian's every whim—
I mean, the lotus position's dead easy for 'im!

And I found affirmations a bit 'ard to take
Despite what I said, me mind knew it was false
It's really much more than a bloke can endure
'Cos I only came 'ere for some magical cure.

The remedy prescribed by their 'Dr Macrae'
Was a 'meditation cocktail'—taken four times a day.
But we have no doubt, as we sift through all this chaff
The best medicine of all is a bloody good laugh!

Grace's quite amazing . . . she's real living proof
Of the value in dryin' yer grapes on the roof.
But I asked her one question I'm sorry she anser'd—

No bloke likes to 'ear that 'is nuts 'ave gone rancid!

Now the group of us 'ere—we're not such a bad lot
But we've all now damn near 'ad enough of this rot;
One more day in this place and we'd surely revolt . . .
I'd give me right arm for a spoonful of salt.

So if yer riddled with cancer and you've lost all yer drive
And ya really see no point in stayin' alive
Don't go to the Gawlers, 'cos no matter 'ow 'ard ya try
They'll 'ave ya stay 'ealthy
Till the day that ya die!

Trevor Steele—August 1986

Index

Dorothy Edgelow and Lynette Archer
can be contacted at The Foundation.
Details on Dr Ian Gawler's work with
The Gawler Foundation are available by contacting:

The Gawler Foundation
P.O. Box 77G, Yarra Junction, Victoria 3797 Australia
Phone: (03) 5967 1730 or Fax: (03) 5967 1715
International Dialling: + 61 3 5967 1730
Email: info@gawler.asn.au

BOOKS, TAPES & CDs

**Ian Gawler has prepared the following tapes and CDs with exercises
to support your practise of the techniques described in this book**

Books
You Can Conquer Cancer
   New Edition
Peace of Mind
Meditation Pure and Simple
The Creative Power of Imagery

The Meditation Tapes
MT1:   Integral Meditation: How to Meditate — Theory & Exercises.
MT2:   Relaxation & Meditation: Relaxing deeply and quickly.
MT3:   Deepening Your Meditation: Using breath and sound.
MT4:   Meditation — Pure & Simple: Exercises for stilling the mind.
         These four tapes are available singly or as a set.

The Imagery Tapes
IT1:   The Power of the Mind: Positive Affirmations & Imagery.
IT2:   Guided Imagery: The Healing Journey and White Light Exercises.
IT3:   Inner Peace, Inner Wisdom: The Quiet Place & Inner Guide Exercises.
IT4:   Making Peace: The Art of Forgiveness with Exercises.
         These four tapes are available singly or as a set.

The CDs
CD1:   Relaxation, Meditation and Imagery: Rapid Relaxation, Progressive Muscle Relaxation
         and White Light Exercises
CD2:   Meditation — Pure & Simple: Exercises for Stilling the Mind

Meditation, Imagery and Music
From Sound Into Silence — CD & Tape — consisting of:
      Deep Relaxation — The Progressive Muscle Relaxation
      The Inner Journey — A Guided Imagery
      *In which Ian is joined by the harp and singing of Peter
      Roberts, to add another dimension to these exercises.*

Other tapes are available on topics relating to lifestyle, health, healing and wellbeing.
For a brochure or to order directly, contact the Foundation at the above address.